China Toothpick Holders

Judy Knauer
and Sandra Raymond

Schiffer Publishing Ltd

4880 Lower Valley Road, Atglen, PA 19310 USA

Designed by Mark David Bowyer
Type set in University Roman Bd BT/Dutch801 Rm BT

ISBN: 0-7643-2045-9
Printed in China
1 2 3 4

Published by Schiffer Publishing Ltd.
4880 Lower Valley Road
Atglen, PA 19310
Phone: (610) 593-1777; Fax: (610) 593-2002
E-mail: Info@schifferbooks.com

For the largest selection of fine reference books on this and
related subjects, please visit our web site at
www.schifferbooks.com
We are always looking for people to write books on new and
related subjects. If you have an idea for a book please
contact us at the above address.

This book may be purchased from the publisher.
Include $3.95 for shipping.
Please try your bookstore first.
You may write for a free catalog.

In Europe, Schiffer books are distributed by
Bushwood Books
6 Marksbury Ave.
Kew Gardens
Surrey TW9 4JF England
Phone: 44 (0) 20 8392-8585; Fax: 44 (0) 20 8392-9876
E-mail: info@bushwoodbooks.co.uk
Free postage in the U.K., Europe; air mail at cost.

Contents

Acknowledgments 4

Introduction 5

How To Use this Reference 7

History of Toothpick Holders 8

Manufacturing China Toothpick Holders 10

Collecting China Toothpick Holders 12

About Prices 16

How this Reference is Organized 17

Toothpick Holders by Point of Origin 18

    Austria 18

    Bavaria 19

        Royal Bayreuth 23

    Czechoslovakia 49

    England 51

        Royal Doulton 59

    France 63

    Germany 66

        Silesia 72

        Unmarked 75

        Carnival Lustre 86

        Elfinware 87

    Japan (Nippon) 87

    Prussia 102

    United States 124

Souvenir Toothpick Holders 127

Sanitary Toothpick Holders 131

Figural Toothpick Holders 137

    Pink Pigs 144

Miscellaneous Toothpick Holders 146

Contemporary Toothpick Holders 157

Match Holders 159

Appendix 162

Glossary 171

Bibliography 173

Index 174

Acknowledgments

One of the most difficult aspects of preparing a collector's reference book such as this is the inability to have all of the items in one place, at one time, so you can group them appropriately for photographs. One of the most pleasant and most rewarding aspects of creating this book has been the wonderful, generous cooperation we have received from the many friends, collectors, and dealers who willingly shared their knowledge and their collections with us, some of whom were so eager to contribute to the publication of information on china toothpick holders that they trusted us with their treasures, without even knowing us!

A special thank you goes to those who made us welcome in their homes and allowed us to photograph items from their collections. This includes Lee and Helen L. Boyd, "Red" and Betty Edwards, Barbara Elliott, Dale and Joyce Ender, and Liz Hartman. We also photographed many toothpick holders from the collections belonging to Iva Bader, Rose E. Beach, John Conner, Robert and Kathy DeWitt, June L. Fossey, Ted Friesner, Sarah Jenkins, Dorlis G. Kohler, Mary Ann Kolb, Bobbi Levan, Carmania Lewis, Leland Marple, Paul and Jane Parker, Jo and Bob Sanford, C & J Snape of Golden Goose Antiques, Leo and Pauline Soderholm, Alene Stoner, Carol Trego, Rich Trunkey, Harry and Nancy Ware, and Katharyn and Phil Yonge. We appreciate each and every one of you and could not have completed this book without your help.

We would also like to thank the staff at Schiffer Publishing for their assistance and for the patience and supportive manner in which it was given. Ginny Parfitt provided amazing help and guidance in the final formatting and always had answers to our seemingly impossible questions. A special thank you goes to our editor, Doug Congdon-Martin, who was always available and who went above and beyond to assure our successful completion of the book. We appreciate your encouragement and help, Doug.

And last, but most certainly not least, Sandra would especially like to thank her husband, Jim, "He always supports my obsessions. I could not have done this endeavor without his encouragement and patience."

Introduction

As long-time active collectors of antique toothpick holders, we have often been stymied in our search to identify the beautiful china and porcelain toothpick holders we have added to our collections. We have found that there are a number of excellent references on glass toothpick holders, but very little is available on china pieces. And what is available is found in references that focus on a specific type of china. That means a collector might have to search through a dozen different books before finding anything related to the toothpick holder they are trying to identify – and may not find anything even then.

Glass toothpick holders can often be identified by their pattern name and/or their manufacturer. The same is not generally true for china toothpick holders. Many of them carry no manufacturer's mark, and the variety of shapes and decorations is endless. The majority of the shapes and decorations are not named. And yet, we do not want to overlook these little gems. Many of them are miniature works of art!

While "ceramic" is the generic name for the majority of molded products made from clay, and the technically correct term for most of the toothpick holders featured in this reference is "porcelain," we have chosen to use the more commonly accepted term, "china." One can check the Glossary for a more detailed description of the distinctions among the various types of clay-based wares. We have also decided to use the term "toothpicks" instead of "toothpick holders." This is consistent with how collectors refer to them – and it's shorter!

Our primary objective is to show you a wide variety of toothpicks, from a wide range of sources, and provide as much information about them as possible. It is our hope that this will provide you with additional information on your collection and thus enhance the pleasure of collecting. We also hope this reference will facilitate communication about this collectible and draw out more information that surely exists.

While it would be impossible to include every china toothpick, we have made a concerted effort to represent the gamut that exists. There are a few categories where we have attempted to provide an example of every known shape or decoration. For example, Royal Bayreuth produced a wide variety of recognizable patterns and shapes. We have tried to represent as many of these as possible. Many of the R. S. Prussia and R. S. Germany decorations are unnamed, but many of the molds are numbered and/or named, so we have tried to include as many of the shapes as possible. We have also included sketches of the various shapes of which we are aware. This will assist you in identifying Prussian toothpicks that are not marked.

Now, having said that you can identify toothpicks by their shape, we are going to introduce a caveat. It was not uncommon for popular shapes and decorations to be copied, making it a little more difficult to distinguish between a more valuable toothpick and one of lesser quality. For example, we have provided a photograph comparing a fine quality, three-handled R. S. Prussia (RSP) toothpick holder with one from Japan that is very similar in shape (See Fig. 4). When you spot this toothpick holder sitting alone in an antique shop, you may need to take a closer look to determine if it is the more valuable RSP or the lesser quality Japanese version. This is not to imply that the Japanese produced an inferior product. Quite to the contrary, their wares range from lesser quality to very fine items produced primarily for export. They, more than any other country, can boast that the majority of their wares were hand painted.

We also know that the exact same mold can be found with different manufacturers' marks. This might indicate that the molds were sold by one factory to another; that the undecorated blanks were sold to various manufacturing and decorating firms that decorated them and then applied their mark; or that a company produced wares for other companies. Royal Bayreuth is one example of the latter possibility. Fig. 136 shows a mark used on a tapestry toothpick holder made by Royal Bayreuth (Porcelain Factory, Tettau), but marked Gobelin Ware to represent the company that commissioned the work and sold or distributed the wares.

We have included a few figural toothpicks, but not many because that could be another complete book. Also, many small figurals made with a holder or small container are not really toothpicks.

There are many items that are very similar to and often confused with toothpicks. We have tried to exclude these, except as examples for comparison purposes. You will find additional comment on this as well as the criteria we used in determining what is and what is not a toothpick holder in the Collecting China Toothpick Holders chapter.

We have included a brief section on contemporary toothpicks with the objective of showing you those that we feel might be confused with the antique toothpicks. More modern ceramic and novelty toothpicks have not been included.

It is our hope that providing this reference will be a first step in sharing information about antique china toothpicks. We know that our information will be far from complete and we hope that if you have additional information, you will share that with us. We are especially interested in hearing about previously un-attributed tooth-picks that you may have with an identifying mark. We plan to document any new findings and mail updates to our readers periodically. Contact information is included with the authors' biographies. Please use this means to send us any additional information and to be added to our contact list.

How to Use this Reference

China toothpick holders tend to be known by the name of their manufacturer or their place of origin. Only a small percentage of them actually have a pattern name associated with them. Add to that the fact that many of them carry no markings to assist in their identity, and you have a real research challenge!

In trying to make this reference as easy to navigate as possible, we have created a section for each country or region that created the examples shown in this book, realizing that the course of history has changed some of these names. We did this because, while some toothpick holders are stamped with the manufacturer's mark, there are many examples marked only for the region or country in which they originated. Also, many manufacturer marks include the name of the country or region. Basing the organization of this book on point of origin should make it easy for you to find information on those items that carry some kind of backstamp or mark.

Some chapters are further divided into groupings by manufacturer and/or by region. For example, the chapter on English toothpick holders will include a selection of Royal Doulton toothpicks. Bavaria, a region within the German Empire, produced a large number of toothpicks and will have its own chapter. Most chapters will also include some unmarked toothpick holders that, through our research, we can reasonably attribute to that country.

We have included as many manufacturer's marks as possible from the many toothpick holders we have had the pleasure of examining and photographing. If you have a toothpick holder with only a partial mark or one that is indistinguishable, you may be able to compare it with the examples provided and determine its origin.

If you are trying to identify an unmarked toothpick holder from your collection, or perhaps one that has been in your family, you may not find that exact one pictured, but you should be able to leaf through this book and find examples that are similar in shape, design, and other characteristics.

We have included separate chapters for sanitary (horizontal) toothpicks and for figurals. Again, this was done to facilitate your searching for a particular item.

There is a Miscellaneous chapter that shows a variety of unmarked and un-attributed toothpick holders. If you happen to have any of these in your collection and they are marked, we would love to hear from you so the information we have provided can be updated.

At the very end of the book, you will find a small section on contemporary toothpicks, examples of match holders that are often included in collections, a glossary of terms used throughout this reference, a bibliography, and an index.

We have tried to provide as much information as possible about the toothpicks shown in the book. We encourage you to read both the introduction to each section and the caption provided with each photograph to get complete information. We have not included dimensions for the toothpicks since most are 2 1/4" tall, give or take 1/4". A pedestal or feet will obviously add to the overall height. We have tried to make note of those that are smaller or larger than the typical toothpick.

History of Toothpick Holders

Toothpick holders became popular in the United States about 1885 and although their popularity waned after 1910, many continued to be manufactured or imported through the 1930s and 1940s. Many glass toothpicks were produced here in the United States, but the vast majority of china toothpicks were imported. Germany and Japan produced them in vast quantities, and often specifically for the export trade. Visit the home of any elderly relative today and you are likely to find a toothpick carefully preserved in the back of the china closet. They were that popular! Every home had at least one.

Toothpicks were often made as a component of a complete table service. Think about the many Limoges and Old Ivory patterns you have seen. Many of them included a toothpick holder that was passed around at the end of the meal. They were, after all, a necessary part of a well-set table along with spoon holders, salt dips, knife rests, butter pats, and celery vases. Just think how that compares to the way we set a table today!

You will also find that many toothpicks were made as part of a condiment set. A condiment set typically included a salt shaker, pepper shaker, and toothpick holder on a small tray. Sometimes a mustard jar was included.

The etiquette surrounding the use of the actual "toothpick" is quite interesting. During their heyday, it was considered quite proper to pass the toothpick holder around the table so guests could use the toothpicks to clean their teeth. Later, it was determined that when one "picked" their teeth at the table, it should be done behind the discreet cover of a linen napkin. Today, we are more likely to make toothpicks available to guests in need, once they are away from the dinner table. In some Asian countries, picking ones teeth after eating is quite expected, but both hands must be used – one to operate the pick and the other to politely cover your mouth.

The actual "toothpick" – the item used to clean ones teeth after a meal – has evolved over the years. Its history is both crude and elegant. The use of toothpicks to clean the teeth is one of the earliest customs documented. It is known that they were in use well before the time of Christ. Early toothpicks were made from pieces of bone or the stem of a feather (quill). People of wealth would have toothpicks made of gold, silver, or ivory and they might be inlaid with precious stones. They were such an important and valued tool that they were often considered heirlooms. When the infanta Louise Marie Therese of Parma married a prince, her dowry included "a dozen valuable toothpicks." It is said that the prophet Muhammad had a servant called the "master of the toothpick" and his primary responsibility was to care for Muhammad's valuable toothpick! We know that our Victorian ancestors generally carried personal toothpicks. Often made of gold or silver, a gentleman's toothpick might have a gem stone embedded in one end and he carried it in his pocket. A lady's toothpick might have a ring on one end so the tool could be attached to a chatelaine or worn on a chain around her neck.

Today, we use the humble wooden toothpicks and the ritual of cleaning ones teeth is usually done in private. But even our wooden toothpicks have a history as shown in the photographs below.

Fig. 1. An old box of wooden toothpicks labeled LaMarquise Orange Wood Toothpicks, Made in Germany. The writing on the outside of the box is in English, leading us to wonder if these were made for export.

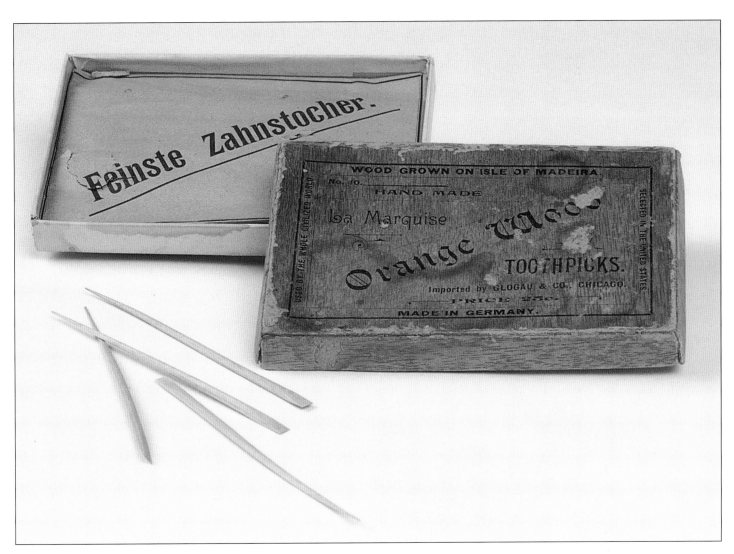

Fig. 2. The toothpicks are tapered at one end and are 4" long. It is interesting to note
that the labeling on the tissue they are wrapped in is written in German.

Manufacturing China Toothpick Holders

Without going into a technical description of the various formulas and the manufacturing process, we are going to provide just the basic steps involved in creating china dinnerware. Yes, we admit to over simplifying, but feel that the average collector would not carry their research to greater depths. For those who are interested in additional information, there are many excellent references available, including *Bohemian Decorated Porcelain,* by Dr. James D. Henderson, listed in our Bibliography.

The basic ingredients used in the manufacturing of ceramics are kaolin, quartz, and feldspar. Kaolin is a fine-grained clay of high quality, free from iron and other impurities. In most cases, the ceramic industry developed in those areas where the finest kaolin could be found. Once the ingredients have been cleaned and prepared, they are mixed with water. If the item is to be turned on a potter's wheel, the mixture is made thick enough so the potter can shape the clay into the desired form. If the item is to be molded – as nearly all toothpicks are – the mixture or "slip" is made thin enough that it can be poured into a plaster mold. Plaster was used for the molds because it would absorb the moisture from the slip. As the slip dried, it pulled away from the mold. The object would then be placed in a kiln along with other objects and be fired for the first time. This firing removed still more moisture, leaving the piece hardened enough for easy handling. The resulting product is still quite brittle and porous, enabling it to easily accept a liquid glaze. This initial glaze was typically a thinner version of the slip used originally. The item is then fired again to adhere the glaze and give a smooth, hard finish to the object. The product or blank is now hard and white, very near the appearance of a finished piece of china. The item is ready for decoration at this point and, depending on the type of product being produced, it may undergo additional glazing and firing.

The most common ways of applying the decoration to the toothpicks are by hand painting and by transfer (decal), or a combination of the two methods. You might think that the hand painted toothpicks would be of greater value, but this is not necessarily the case. For example, the prices paid for Nippon toothpicks rarely come close to those paid for Royal Bayreuth, yet the Nippon is hand painted and the Royal Bayreuth decorations are primarily decals.

Early transfer work was done by creating the master design on paper, then punching numerous pin holes along each line of the design. The design was then placed over the object being decorated and patted with graphite. The fine graphite would leave an outline on the item that the decorators could then follow as they painted the object. This was a very time consuming process and factories began looking for an easier way to apply decorations that could be repeated on many pieces of porcelain. By the time toothpicks came into vogue, the trade had perfected colored decal-like transfers that could be applied directly to the porcelain. For this reason, the terms "transfer" and "decal" are often used synonymously by those who collect items manufactured in the late 1800s and beyond.

Sometimes the difference between hand painting and transfer work is obvious, but other times it can be difficult to determine. There are several ways to identify transfer work. Applying a flat transfer to a curved object can be difficult, so look for folds or overlaps in the decals, especially along the outside edges. Sometimes when looking very closely you can detect small tears at the edges of decals, or you may notice a design that ends abruptly at the edge of a decal. If the decal wraps all the way around the toothpick, you may actually see where it overlaps. Royal Bayreuth and Old Ivory are examples of well-known toothpicks that are decorated using decals.

When the decoration is done by hand, you may notice variations in the thickness of the enamel or be able to feel the texture of the paint when you run your fingers across the design. If you have the opportunity to see two examples of the same pattern side-by-side, you will note variations in the design, even though the over-all design is the same. Fig. 295 shows three Japanese toothpicks that are basically the same shape and design, and that are highly decorated with red and gold, yet the variations in the design are quite obvious.

Royal Bayreuth and Old Ivory are excellent examples of the use of both methods of decorating. The background on the Royal Bayreuth toothpicks is hand painted and may vary from one to another even though the transfer used is the same. For example, one may have a single colored background with just a little mottling effect while another bearing the same transfer may show a farm scene. The greater the detail of the background, the more valuable the item. With the Old Ivory, the background is hand painted ivory and the various trims are hand painted using gold and brown. After the decal is applied, it is often "touched up" by adding a little enamel. For example, touching up the outline of the flowers gives them more of a hand painted look.

The decoration can be applied before the item is glazed (underglaze) or afterward (overglaze). The decoration will withstand wear and use better if it is applied before the glaze and has the glaze as a protective coating. One way to tell the difference between underglaze and overglaze is to lightly run your fingertips over the decorated surface. If the decoration has been applied under the glaze, the surface will be smooth and even in texture. When you look at the item in a bright light, the reflection from the decorated area will be the same as that from the undecorated area. Conversely, when the overglaze process is used, you should be able to feel different textures and perhaps detect a difference in the thickness of the paint or feel the edge of a decal. When you look at the item in bright light, the reflection from the decorated area will be different than that from the undecorated area.

Other ways of decorating toothpicks are through the application of a surface treatment or by applying molded porcelain shapes, making the surface three dimensional. Surface finishes can include various types of lustre, a matte or dull finish, a sanded or grainy texture, or a linen-like tapestry finish. The application of shapes made from porcelain can be seen in Elfinware, what we have chosen to call Carnival Lustre, and other items that may have a bird, flower, or berry attached.

Collecting China Toothpick Holders

If you are already collecting china toothpick holders, you probably know just how quickly a collection of this small item can grow into something much larger than you anticipated. If you are a beginning collector, you may be confused about what to collect and how to go about finding your collectibles. We will provide some ideas and suggestions based on our experience and what we have learned from collector friends. By putting this information in a question and answer format, we hope you will be able to focus on the questions that interest you.

Where will I find toothpick holders?

While china toothpicks are still readily available, it is unlikely that you will find many in one place with the possible exception of the online auctions. There, you can perform a search and come up with quite a list! Read the descriptions carefully, though. Returning unwanted purchases can be very costly and time consuming, not to mention frustrating. Verify that the toothpick is free of damage and that the shipping charges are reasonable.

Check out your local antique shops and malls, and talk to the dealers. They can sometimes provide leads that you may otherwise be unaware of. They may even know someone who has some for sale. Antique shows are another good source. There, you often find the better quality toothpicks. Check your newspaper for listings of estate auctions being held in the area. Even if the listing does not include toothpicks, there is a good possibility they will have one or two to sell. If you have the time and enjoy the exercise, flea markets and garage sales are sometimes a good place to scout out bargains. They are full of surprises!

When you travel, plan to allow a couple of extra hours so you can visit antique shops while taking your rest breaks. And, don't forget your relatives. The next time you visit Great Aunt Bertha, ask if she has a toothpick holder in her china cabinet. She just might!

And last, but certainly not least, if you are a member of the National Toothpick Holder Collectors Society, you will find "for sale" ads regularly in the Toothpick Bulletin and you will find literally hundreds for sale at the annual convention. Membership provides a great opportunity to network with other collectors – many of whom have duplicates they are eager to sell or trade. Membership information is provided later in this chapter.

How do I know which ones are "good"?

You can typically tell the quality of a toothpick by examining the porcelain and the decoration. Better quality porcelain will be whiter in color and have minimum imperfections. The finish will be hard and evenly applied. The item is generally thinner and may have a translucent quality. When you tap good quality porcelain, you hear a clear ring, much as you do with crystal. Lesser quality items tend to be thicker and the porcelain may have a gray or bluish cast. Imperfections, such as small stones, black inclusions, and gaps in the glaze are often visible on items of lesser quality. When you tap these items with your fingernail, the sound will be dull and flat.

When examining the decoration, look at the level of detail and the quality of the work. This would apply to both hand-painted toothpicks and those decorated with transfers, which are frequently designed by artists. Consider the amount of decoration. An all-over floral design would require more of an artist's effort than a toothpick that simply has a band of color around it. The use of gold is another indication of quality. Gold is not generally applied to an item intended to retail at a low price.

How can I distinguish a Toothpick Holder from other small items?

So many antique and collectible categories are plagued with a myriad of reproductions that seduce collectors with their beauty, availability, and potential. Perhaps we are fortunate as collectors of china toothpicks in that there are only a few reproductions and fakes of which we need to be aware. You will find information on these throughout this reference.

But that is not the end of the story. We have other issues with which to contend. Many other issues! There are so many other items that are similar to toothpicks that it is sometimes difficult to be certain of what we are buying. If you have ever purchased items for your collection by mail, you may have been the recipient of one of these "wanna bees." If you have searched for toothpick holders on the online auction services, you certainly have seen a few examples!

Here is a list: shot glasses, small open sugars, egg cups, creamers, fairings, small vases, match holders, figurines, card holders, cigarette holders, novelties, decorative cups, children's dishes, wine glasses, and wine glasses with the stems neatly removed. You can probably add some others.

While we do admit to exceptions to every rule, we generally feel that if you put a toothpick (a real one) in the holder and it falls over or drops out of sight, the item is probably not a toothpick holder. One notable exception is the Royal Bayreuth toothpick holders which tend to be larger – but then, toothpicks used to be larger, too, as shown in Fig. 2. Here are some other guidelines we use in establishing our definition of a toothpick holder.

If…	It is probably…
it has a pour spout and handle…	a pitcher or creamer.
it has a single handle…	a cup, no matter how ornate.
the interior is not cylindrical…	not a toothpick holder.
the opening is less than an inch wide…	not a toothpick holder.
the opening is more than 2 1/4" wide…	not a toothpick holder.
the opening is less than 1 1/2" deep…	not a toothpick holder.
it has an obvious "striker"…	a match holder.
it is wall mounted…	a match holder.
the inside flows into the shape of the item…	not a toothpick holder.
the opening is the shape of the narrow end of an egg…	an egg cup.
it has a small opening and a wide body…	a small vase.
it is oblong rather than cylindrical…	a holder for calling cards or a cigarette holder.

How much should I spend?

This is a personal decision that each of us must make based on our financial situation. Creating a budget assures that you are not over spending on your hobby. Collecting can become a passion, and since we have not yet found an Antiques Anonymous group, it is best to have a budget and stay within it.

As for how much to spend on any individual toothpick, that again is a personal decision and depends on what you decide to collect and your objectives. If you are collecting as an investment, you will undoubtedly want to focus on the more valuable toothpicks. If you are collecting strictly for pleasure, your personal preferences and your budget should be used in making this decision. We know people who have set a limit of $25 per toothpick and stick to it. Their collections include some very fine pieces that they have found at bargain prices, but they are not likely to amass a valuable collection.

How can I limit my collection? Should I specialize? I'm getting so many!

If you have been collecting for a while or have limited space for displaying the toothpicks, specializing is a good idea. But how do you choose what to collect?

Beauty is truly in the eye of the beholder. Which toothpicks do you like the best? Which purchases have you been so excited about that you couldn't wait to tell a friend? How you answer these questions might provide a clue as to what you should collect. There are a number of ways to limit your collection by focusing in one direction. Here are some possibilities:

Collect toothpicks with a certain characteristic. For example, you might collect only those with feet, with handles, with a floral decoration, with advertising or souveniring, with a lustre finish, with a tapestry finish, or with a portrait on them.

Collect toothpicks made by a certain manufacturer or from a specific location. Options in this category could include Royal Bayreuth, R. S. Prussia, or Royal Doulton. You could collect toothpicks made in Japan, Germany, Bavaria, England, or Austria.

Should I keep an inventory of my collection?

Yes, definitely yes! The benefits of keeping an inventory are many. First of all, it provides a quick reference as to what you have in your collection and how much you are spending. It is also very important if you want to insure your collection. Later, if you decide to sell all or part of your collection, or if that honor (responsibility!) is left to your heirs, it can be used as a guide in determining the value of each individual toothpick.

Your inventory should include as much descriptive information about the toothpick as possible (pattern or mold name, manufacturer, unique characteristics), the amount you paid, the date of purchase, and a note as to where this toothpick is included in reference books and the value placed on it. Ideally, a picture of each toothpick would be included.

Then, just for fun, you might want to document where you made the purchase, the circumstances under which the toothpick was purchased, and any known history related to the toothpick. We have toothpicks with notes in them detailing who received the toothpick originally and how it was passed through the family. Many a collector has taken nostalgic trips down memory lane just by reading though their inventory.

How can I display them when I have so many?

Displaying toothpicks can be a real challenge since they are all similar in size. You may decide that it would be worth having shallow display cases made if you consider yourself a serious collector. If you are displaying them in a china cabinet, a curio, or a bookcase, stepped shelves can be very effective. You can buy stepped shelves made out of acrylic specifically for displaying small items. An inexpensive option is to purchase the spice racks sold through kitchen specialty shops or catalogs. These are usually white plastic and can be expanded to different widths. Spice racks have an advantage over the molded acrylic, which makes them especially good for curio cabinets. They can be placed in the cabinet before expanding them to the desired width, and the white color provides a pleasing background.

Shadow boxes and knick-knack shelves are nice for small collections, but we find you can outgrow them very quickly. They can be used most effectively as decorating accents in a room. For example, you could display a collection of blue and white toothpicks in your kitchen.

Are china toothpick holders still being made?

Yes, but they are not like the old ones that were carefully manufactured with ornate handles and then intricately decorated by a staff of professional artists. Any grocery or variety store will offer several, with the most common being the ceramic figurals. You will frequently find toothpicks anywhere souvenir items are sold. And they are still a favorite among china painters.

Be sure to review the chapter on Contemporary Toothpick Holders.

How can I learn more about the toothpicks I have?

You have taken the first step by purchasing this book. There are other books available that include china toothpicks along with those made of glass or metal. These are listed in the bibliography. If you collect a specific type of toothpick, there may be reference books for that collectible. For example, if you collect Japanese toothpicks, there are a number of references available on Nippon and Noritake.

The Toothpick Bulletin published by the National Toothpick Holder Collectors Society includes information on toothpicks of all kinds. Membership also provides the opportunity to ask questions through the Bulletin, or by networking with other members.

A reliable, experienced, antique dealer is another good source of information. The periodical catalog at your local library would be a good source for articles on toothpicks that have appeared in the various antique-related publications.

It is our hope that you and other readers will provide feedback to us, so that we can add to the information in this book and share it with other collectors. Perhaps you have information on some of the toothpicks that we were unable to document as to source or origin.

Do I need to worry about reproductions?

Actually, reproductions are less of an issue with china toothpicks than they are with most collectibles, but there are a couple of precautions we would like to mention. Since toothpick holders are still being made, you need to be familiar with what is new. Most of the ceramic and novelty toothpicks currently available are inexpensively made and are easy to identify. Most are imported from Japan or Taiwan.

The blanks used for china painting present a bit more of a problem. Some of them are similar in shape to antique toothpicks and, because they are hand decorated, they can look a lot like the old ones. We show most of these shapes in the chapter called Contemporary Toothpick Holders. We suggest that you review that chapter and become familiar with the shapes.

Of real concern are the fake marks that are being used on contemporary toothpicks. There are several fake Nippon marks on the market, but we know of only one that has been found on toothpick holders. An example of that one, the Maple Leaf mark, is shown in Fig. 294 in the chapter on Japan (Nippon). Fake R. S. Prussia marks are also being applied to contemporary toothpicks. An example of this mark can be seen in Fig. 359 in the Prussia chapter. By becoming familiar with the shapes of the contemporary toothpicks, you may save yourself the disappointment of buying a new toothpick thinking it is old.

One other word of caution. As we mentioned before, some of the newer toothpicks are very similar to the older ones, and some older ones are similar enough to be confusing. Please note the two examples below.

Fig. 3. Two very similar molds, but the one on the left is old and the one on the right is new. The old one has more pronounced variations on the top rim, more distinct feet created from the rays on the underside, and is slightly smaller. The new one has more bulk and the feet are less obvious. The old one is marked "Richter, Bavaria" with a shield and crown. This same mold is known to have been made as a souvenir item and marked "Germany."

Fig. 4. Another example of two similar, but different molds. In this case, both are old but they are made in different countries. The toothpick on the left is a three-handled Reinhold Schlegelmilch Prussia (RSP) mold. To recognize this mold, look for the small knobs on top of the handles and the fan-like embossing that stretches from the six scallops at the top to an elongated "V" that ends at the base. The one on the right is a three-handled Japanese mold. The top of the handles is smooth and the top rim has very shallow scallops with three serrations between each of the handles. A third variation of this mold comes from Austria. It is similar to the Japanese mold but is thinner porcelain and the three serrations are more pronounced.

Should I insure my collection?

Check with the agent who handles your homeowner's insurance or your apartment content policy. That is generally easier than trying to read the policy! Ask how much coverage your current policy includes for your toothpicks and the types of disasters that are covered. If you are comfortable that your collection is sufficiently covered, no additional coverage is necessary. You can consult your inventory to determine the approximate value of your collection.

However, if you find that the coverage is not sufficient – which is most often the case, ask what additional coverage is available and the rate for that coverage. Most collectibles are covered under a Fine Arts rider. You will also want to ask what kind of documentation they require as proof of the value of your collection. They may require that the collection be appraised by a professional appraiser, or they may allow you to provide a listing along with current book values.

Should I buy toothpicks that are damaged?

As a general rule, we say "no" to damaged toothpicks, especially if you are buying as an investment. There are some exceptions, however. If you find a very rare toothpick, one that you are not likely to have the opportunity to purchase again in the near future and the damage is minimal, buy it. You should expect to pay much less than book value for a damaged item. Also, if you are collecting for pleasure and do not object to small nicks, weigh the cost against how much you like the toothpick holder. You may decide the damage is insignificant.

Is there a collector's club for toothpick holder collectors?

Yes, there is, and we are glad you asked! The National Toothpick Holder Collectors Society (NTHCS) is an active group of approximately eight hundred members from across the United States and Canada. They publish ten Toothpick Bulletins a year and hold an annual convention in August. The society was founded by Judy Knauer in 1973, and its membership includes both novice and experienced collectors. The society has sponsored several books on toothpick holders and has had a number of exclusive toothpick holders made for their annual conventions, which are held at various locations throughout the United States.

For membership information, please contact the current Membership Chairperson at NTHCS, P. O. Box 852, Archer City, TX 76351. Membership information is also available from the authors or by visiting the society's web site at www.NTHCS.org.

About Prices

Price guides – a necessary evil! You use them, we use them, collectors and dealers use them, and our publisher requires them. They are probably the most difficult part of writing a book and often become the topic of heated discussions among readers. We wonder if any writers have ever been told they did a great price guide. Doubtful.

There are many reasons why the guides are difficult to create and why there is so much dissention over prices. It is definitely not an exact science! Prices vary from one part of the country to another, as well as from one collectible to another. For example, the value a Nippon collector places on a Nippon toothpick may be very different than the value a toothpick collector places on that very same toothpick. We have also learned that those who specialize in a particular type or style of toothpick tend to value those higher than any other. It is next to impossible to be objective about the items that we own and that are very special to us. Which leads to another point – just because an avid collector pays $500 for something they "can't live without" or "have never seen before," that does not mean the item is worth $500. It only means that particular buyer was willing to pay that particular amount to become the owner of that particular item. Right? We are all probably guilty of over paying at some time or another, just to get something our heart desired.

If we look at prices in general, we see that they have been lower the past couple of years. The economy has been a major contributor to that. While we like to think in terms of "needing" an item for our collection, the truly honest must admit that these items are not necessities and those most affected by the waning economy have limited their buying. A second key factor is the Internet. Thanks to Internet dealers and online auctions, items it might have taken us years to find are now available at the click of a mouse.

There are many factors related directly to the toothpicks themselves that impact price. A toothpick that is especially beautiful in decoration and/or shape will command a higher price than one of similar quality and origin that is perceived as being less attractive. Rarity is also a factor. While the price range for most Royal Bayreuth toothpicks may be between $150 and $350, a very rare figural will sell for much more than that. And, just as we pay more for brand-name clothing, known names associated with china toothpicks also command a higher price. Think of Royal Bayreuth, R. S. Prussia, Old Ivory, and Wedgwood, for example.

Condition certainly affects price. While most collectors will not mind if the trim shows a little wear (after all, some of the toothpicks have been around for over one hundred years!), a piece in pristine condition will command a higher price. Chips (even small ones) and hairline cracks will most certainly reduce the value of a toothpick. Larger cracks often put the toothpick at risk of breaking and, unless the piece is extremely rare, most collectors will avoid toothpicks that are cracked. This brings to mind a visit to an antique shop in North Carolina many years ago. A delicate, three-handled china toothpick was sitting on a high shelf and, since I could not see the price tag, I asked to see the item and inquired about the price. What a disappointment to see that two of the three handles were badly broken. I was then shocked to see that the price was in excess of $100! When I said, "But, it's broken," the dealer replied, "Yes. But, it's R. S. Prussia."

Back to our price guide. You will find that we have assigned a value range to each toothpick shown. We arrived at this value by consulting with a number of collectors and dealers, and by reviewing many current, existing price guides. We also surfed the Internet and kept notes on prices being asked and prices being paid. Being avid toothpick collectors, we also drew on our own experience gained from many hours of perusing antique malls, antique shops, and antique shows – where very few toothpicks eluded our well trained eyes.

As a final comment, we urge you to use the prices presented here as a guide only. They should not be the sole basis on which you make a buy/don't buy decision. Trust your judgment and your experience, and always ask yourself, "Is this toothpick holder worth that amount to me?"

How this Reference is Organized

This reference arranges toothpick holders into the following chapters:

Toothpick Holders by Point of Origin
    Austria
    Bavaria
    Czechoslovakia
    England
    France
    Germany
    Japan (Nippon)
    Prussia
    United States
    Souvenir Toothpick Holders

Sanitary Toothpick Holders
Figural Toothpick Holders
Miscellaneous Toothpick Holders
Contemporary Toothpick Holders
Match Holders

At the end of the reference you will find an appendix showing line drawings of the Prussian shapes, a glossary of terms related to porcelain and to toothpicks, a bibliography, and an index.

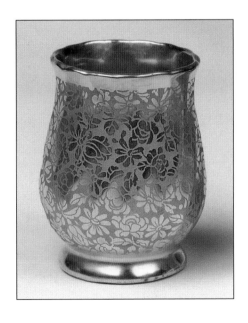

Toothpick Holders by Point of Origin

This chapter is divided into sections that represent the various countries or regions known to have produced a large number of toothpick holders.

Austria

Austrian porcelain rivals German porcelain in quality and, in fact, there are known ties between factories in these two countries. Considering this and the boundary changes in that area of Europe during the 1800s, it is not surprising that research can be confusing. For example, you will find toothpicks marked Carlsbad, Austria and the same mold can be found marked Germany or Czechoslovakia.

Fig. 5. *Left)* Marked – see Fig. 6. $40-50.
Right) Marked – Carlsbad, Made in Austria. $35-45.

Fig. 6. Moritz Zdekauer Porcelain Manufacturer. No date given.

Fig. 7. *Left)* Five sided, sometimes found marked Austria. Unmarked. $40-50. *Center)* Beautiful mold detail, open work at top. Marked – see Fig. 8. $60-70. *Right)* Marked – Austria. $35-45.

Fig. 8. Importer's mark, P.H. Leonard, NY, c. 1908.

Fig. 9. *Left)* Unusual cutout design at top. Marked – see Fig. 10. $45-55. *Center)* Pedestal. Marked – see Fig. 11. $35-45. *Right)* Hand painted. Marked – Austria. $35-45.

Fig. 10. Bawo & Dotter, c. 1884-1914.

Fig. 11. H. Wehinger Horn, c. 1905-1918.

Fig. 12. Silver inside and out.
Marked – Austria. $40-60.

Bavaria

Bavaria, Germany all through the 1800s was the center of that country's porcelain industry. Most pieces found are simply marked "Bavaria," but a few include manufacturer's marks. Famous companies from the region, such as Rosenthal and Hutschenreuther, competed to make beautiful wares for export. Along with their marks, you will find many of the toothpicks have pattern names.

Royal Bayreuth (Tettau Porcelain Manufacturer) is the oldest, privately owned factory in Bavaria.

Fig. 13. *Left)* Very thin porcelain. Marked – see Fig. 25. $60-75. *Right)* Marked – see Fig. 26. $45-55.

Fig. 14. *Left)* Alice pattern. Marked – see Fig. 27. $35-45. *Right)* Cacilie pattern. Marked – see Fig. 27. $35-45.

Fig. 15. *Left)* Charlotte pattern. Marked – see Fig. 27. $40-50. *Center)* Hand painted. Marked – J&C between crossed flower stems, Jaeger & Company, Marktredwitz, Bavaria, c. 1902. $30-40. *Right)* Cacilie pattern. Marked – see Fig. 27. $40-50.

Fig. 16. *Left)* Hexagon shaped. Marked – Bavaria. $30-40.
Center) Same mold as left, with 2 handles. Marked – Bavaria. $35-45.
Right) Ship transfer. Marked – Bavaria. $30-40.

Fig. 17. Hand painted, artist signed Richter. Marked – crown & shield, Bavaria. $45-55.

Fig. 18. Marked – lion over rectangle, Bavaria. $50-60.

Fig. 19. Floral. Marked – lion over rectangle, Bavaria. $35-45.

Fig. 20. Hutschenreuther. *Left)* Madeleine pattern.
Marked – see Fig. 27. $40-50. *Right)* Monbijou
pattern. Marked – see Fig. 27. $40-50.

Fig. 21. Rosenthal. *Left)* Carmen pattern. Marked
– see Fig. 28. $45-55. *Right)* Tilly pattern. Marked
– see Fig. 28. $45-60.

Fig. 22. Rosenthal. Hand painted.
Marked – see Fig. 28. $40-50.

Fig. 23. *Left)* Rosenthal.
Malmaison pattern. Marked –
see Fig. 28. $60-70. *Center)*
Unmarked. Sometimes
marked Rosenthal. $40-50.
Right) Schonwald. Marked –
see Fig. 29. $50-65.

Fig. 24. Seltmann. Swan scene, similar to Prussia swan transfer. Marked – see Fig. 30. $50-65.

Fig. 25. No information found.

Fig. 26. Tirschenreuth Porcelain Factory, Bavaria, c. 1903-1981.

Fig. 27. Hutschenreuther Porcelain Factory, c. 1900. Sometimes found with pattern/mold name over circle. Charlotte shown, other known patterns are Cacili and Alice.

Fig. 28. Rosenthal Porcelain, Bavaria, c. 1891-1907. Sometimes found with pattern/mold name under the crossed swords and crown. Malmaison shown, other known patterns are Tilly, Carmen, Madeleine, and Monbijou.

Fig. 29. Schonwald Porcelain Factory, Schonwald, Bavaria, c. 1911-1927.

Fig. 30. Johann Seltmann, Vohenstrauss, Bavaria (Germany), c. 1901-present.

Royal Bayreuth

Royal Bayreuth wares were produced by the Tettau Porcelain Manufacturer in Bavaria. While there is a town named Bayreuth, the factory is actually located in, and named for the town of Tettau. Their earliest wares are marked with a large capital T and a period. We know of at least one toothpick that carries that mark and that is in their Old Tettau Blue pattern, often referred to as Blue Onion today.

With the exception of the Blue Onion pattern, Royal Bayreuth toothpicks are known for their distinctive shapes and decorations. Once you have become familiar with those, you can easily spot and identify Royal Bayreuth toothpicks, even when they are not marked. Royal Bayreuth toothpicks are generally larger than most other toothpicks, with an average height of approximately 3". Even those with handles and feet tend to have a "sturdy" look rather than a "delicate" appearance.

The decoration typically includes a transfer on a hand-painted background. Background colors vary and sometimes include buildings or a scene. It is not uncommon to find the same transfer used with different backgrounds. You will also notice that many of the transfers can be found facing either to the left or to the right. People and animals were favorite themes for Royal Bayreuth. They are also known for several series that they produced. These include the very popular Sunbonnet Babies, Nursery Rhymes, and Classic or Corinthian Ware.

Royal Bayreuth also made a series of figural toothpick holders, most of which are considered to be quite scarce. You may be familiar with the two most common ones – the Spiky Shell and the Elk.

Tapestry is a unique finish associated with Royal Bayreuth. It is a linen-like surface texture achieved by wrapping the unfinished item in a coarse slip-soaked fabric that was then burned off by the extreme heat used in the manufacturing process. Although other companies produced tapestry, the bulk of it came from the Tettau factory and it is considered to be very desirable. Many shapes and decorations can be found with a tapestry finish, but the most popular by far are the various rose decorations that are known as Rose Tapestry. Highly sought after today, the catalog reprint below shows that these items were relatively inexpensive in 1908.

It is interesting to note that the items marked Royal Bayreuth were produced strictly for export. While that name is familiar to many collectors in the United States, it is virtually unknown in European countries. Tettau wares were not sold locally under the name of Royal Bayreuth.

We have tried to show examples of each shape and each pattern in which Royal Bayreuth toothpicks were made. Shapes known to be missing are the Art Nouveau toothpick holder, one of the coal hod shapes, and a bowl-like shape that extends to form four small feet. We were not able to locate the following patterns: Babes in the Woods, Sunbonnet Babies – Scrubbing (Thursday) and Baking (Saturday), kangaroo, brown bear, or an ivy border.

The Royal Bayreuth photographs that follow are presented in the following order: animals and birds (no people), children (Dutch Children, Nursery Rhymes, Sunbonnet Babies, Sand Babies, Snow Babies), figurals, florals, people (some with animals), and miscellaneous.

No. 83309

Fig. 31. The A. C. McClurg & Co's General Catalogue, 1908-1909, advertises a set of six Royal Bayreuth tapestry toothpick holders, two each of three different designs, for $4.

Animals and Birds

Fig. 32. *Left)* Cows. Unmarked. $250-300. *Right)* Stag in Stream. Unmarked. $300-350.

Fig. 33. Highland Goats. *Left)* Bulbous, four ball feet, no metal rim. Marked – #7. $200-275. *Right)* Three handles. Unmarked. $250-300.

Fig. 34. Highland Sheep. *Left)* Three, flat open tab handles. Unmarked. $250-350. *Right)* Triangular shape with tab handles on sides. Marked – #20 and #27. $200-300.

Fig. 35. Highland Cattle. *Left)* Brown cattle. Unmarked. $200-300. *Right)* Different scene. Marked – see Fig. 131. $200-300.

Fig. 36. *Left)* Rooster and Hen. Marked – #10, #22, and #8. $250-350. *Right)* Black Cow Scene. Unmarked. $250-300.

Fig. 37. Plow Horses. *Left)* Horses with heavy yoke, farm scene background. Unmarked.$250-300. *Right)* Same scene. Unmarked. $250-300.

Fig. 38. The Chase. *Left)* Hounds chasing moose in river, yellow inner rim. Unmarked. $400-500. *Right)* Same scene. Marked – see Fig. 135. $400-450.

Fig. 39. Stag with doe. Three handles meet over top. Marked – see Fig. 135. $350-450.

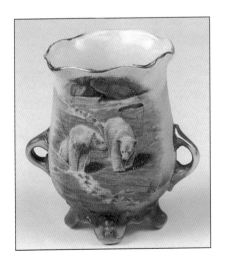

Fig. 40. Polar Bear, tapestry. Rare decoration. Unmarked. $1800-2200.

25

Fig. 41. Frog. Rare decoration, usually found with dark red background. Marked – see Fig. 135. $500-650.

Fig. 42. *Left)* Stork. Different stork on each of the three sides, yellow background. Unmarked. $350-450. *Right)* Penguin. Also known with yellow background. Marked – see Fig. 135. $400-500.

Fig. 43. Swans. Tapestry. *Left)* Two swans on lake. Marked – see Fig. 135. $375-450. *Right)* Same scene. Marked – see Fig. 135. $375-450.

Fig. 44. *Left)* Peacock. Marked – #20 and #3. $375-450. *Right)* Pheasant. Unmarked. $375-450.

Fig. 45. Hoo-poe Bird (various spellings used). Round base pulled out at sides, scarce shape. Marked – see Fig. 135. $400-450.

Fig. 46. *Left)* Blue Bird. Pearlized interior. Unmarked. $300-350. *Right)* Exotic Bird. Two handles, four small, pointed feet. Marked – see Fig. 131. $350-400.

Fig. 47. Exotic Birds. *Left)* With pink floral. Marked – see Fig. 135. $400-450. *Right)* Pair of birds. Marked – #9 and #3. $400-450.

Children

Fig. 48. Dutch Scene. Rare shape, girl with wagon and boy with dog. Marked – see Fig. 135. $350-400.

Fig. 49. Dutch Scene. *Left)* Rare shape, children walking arm in arm. Marked – see Fig. 135. $350-400. *Right)* Children holding hands. Unmarked. $300-350.

Fig. 50. Dutch Scene. *Left)* Children playing with red flag. Unmarked. $300-350. *Right)* Children playing with red flag, three angular handles. Marked – see Fig. 135, #30 and #24. $300-350.

Fig. 51. Dutch Scene. *Left)* Three children holding hands. Unmarked. $300-350. *Right)* Boy and girl with basket on dock. Unmarked. $300-350.

Fig. 52. Dutch Scene. *Left)* Couple skating. Marked – see Fig. 135. $300-350. *Right)* Couple in boat. Marked – see Fig. 135. $300-350.

Fig. 53. Dutch Children. Very rare egg shape with a single handle at top. Marked – see Fig. 135, #8 5/3. $350-400.

Fig. 54. Dutch Scene. *Left)* Woman with two children. Marked – see Fig. 135. $300-350. *Right)* Group of three, windmill in background. Marked – see Fig. 135. $300-350.

Fig. 55. Dutch Scene. *Left)* Group of three, three handles converge over top. Marked – see Fig. 135. $300-350. *Right)* Walking with an umbrella. Marked – see Fig. 135. $300-350.

Fig. 56. Muff Children. Playing with rabbits. Marked – #27 and #68 or #63. $350-400.

Fig. 57. Nursery Rhyme Series. *Left)* Jack and Jill, rhyme on back (may be child's sugar). Unmarked. $450-500. *Right)* Little Jack Horner, rhyme on back. Marked – see Fig. 135. $450-500.

Fig. 58. Nursery Rhyme Series. Reverse of previous photograph, showing the text of the nursery rhymes.

Fig. 59. Nursery Rhyme Series. *Left)* Jack and the Beanstalk. "Jack and the Beanstalk" written in gold. Marked – see Fig. 135. $350-400. *Right)* Little Boy Blue. Rare shape. Marked – see Fig. 135. $375-450.

Fig. 60. Nursery Rhyme Series. *Left)* Little Bo Peep. "Little Bo Peep," rare shape with open work at top. Marked – see Fig. 135. $350-400. *Right)* Little Bo Peep. Kettle shape with handle. Marked – see Fig. 135. $300-350.

Fig. 61. Nursery Rhyme Series. *Left)* Little Miss Muffet. Rare shape with three handles that meet over the top and form flat tabs on the side. "Little Miss Muffet" Marked – see Fig. 135. $400-450. *Right)* Little Boy Blue. Three handles. Marked – see Fig. 135. $350-400.

Fig. 62. Nursery Rhyme Series. *Left)* Ring Around the Rosie. Three handles. Marked – see Fig. 135. $350-400. *Right)* Ring Around the Rosie. Two handles. Marked – see Fig. 135. $350-400.

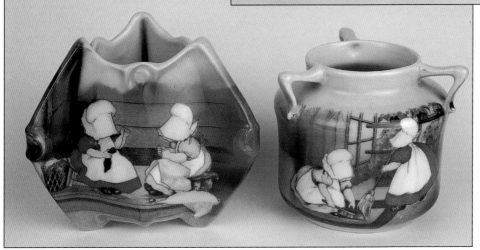

Fig. 63. Sunbonnet Babies. *Left)* Mending (Wednesday), tri-cornered with closed "ears" as handles. Marked – see Fig. 135. $500-600. *Right)* Sweeping (Friday), angular handles. Marked – see Fig. 135. $500-600.

Fig. 64. Sunbonnet Babies. *Left)* Ironing (Tuesday), three handles. Marked – see Fig. 135. $550-650. *Right)* Washing (Monday). Marked – see Fig. 135. $500-600.

Fig. 65. Sunbonnet Babies. Fishing (Sunday). Marked – see Fig. 135. $500-600.

Fig. 66. Sand Babies. *Left)* Unmarked. $350-400. *Right)* Four ball feet and metal rim. Marked – see Fig. 135. $300-375.

Fig. 67. Snow Babies. *Left)* Sledding, similar to sugar bowl, but not sugar bowl. Marked – see Fig. 135. $350-450. *Right)* Ice Play. Marked – see Fig. 135, #95 and #18. $350-400.

Fig. 68. Girl with Dog. *Left)* Two handles. Marked – see Fig. 135. $300-350. *Right)* Rare shape, three flat tab handles. Marked – see Fig. 135. $300-375.

Fig. 69. Children with Puppy and Kitten. *Left)* Very unusual pink background. Unmarked. $350-400. *Right)* Same decoration. Unmarked. $350-450.

Figurals

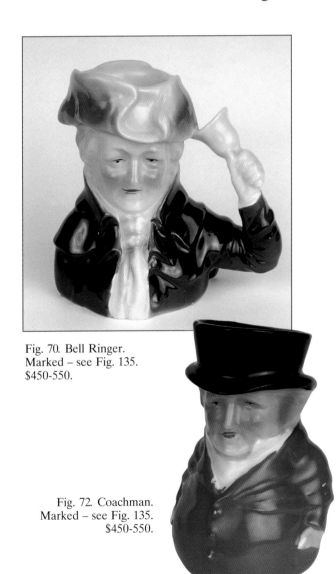

Fig. 70. Bell Ringer. Marked – see Fig. 135. $450-550.

Fig. 72. Coachman. Marked – see Fig. 135. $450-550.

Fig. 71. Clown. Marked – see Fig. 135. $250-350.

Fig. 73. Devil and Cards. Marked – see Fig. 131. $300-400.

Fig. 74. Elk. More common than most of the figurals. Marked – see Fig. 135. $200-250.

Fig. 75. Horse Head, dapple gray, rare, unusual to find it with souveniring, "Ocean City, Md." Marked – T in shield. $450-600.

Fig. 76. Lamp Lighter. Marked – see Fig. 135. $450-550.

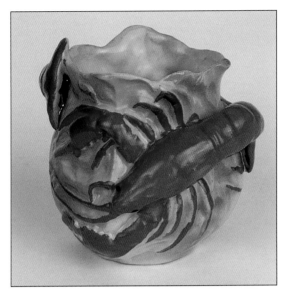

Fig. 77. Lobster and Lettuce. Unmarked. $300-400.

Fig. 78. Oyster Pearl. Amber around top, on handles, and under "skirt," rare. Marked – horse head. $350-450.

Fig. 79. Pansy. Three sided, satin lustre finish. Marked – BAVARIA. $550-700.

Fig. 80. Poppy. Bright red-orange, interior is also decorated. Unmarked. $350-450.

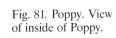

Fig. 81. Poppy. View of inside of Poppy.

Fig. 82. *Left)* Red Pepper. Four lobes with leaves for handles. Unmarked. $325-400. *Right)* Devil. Red match holder with striker on back. Unmarked. $325-400.

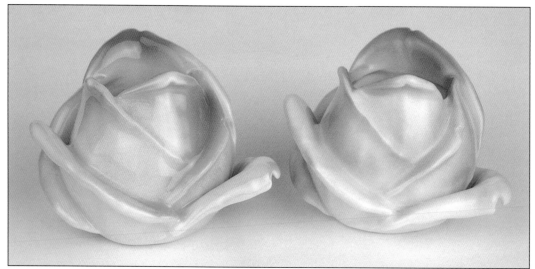

Fig. 83. Rose. *Left)* Rose figural was made in several different colors. Marked – see Fig. 135, plus #26. $350-450. *Right)* Marked – see Fig. 135, #28. $350-450.

Fig. 84. Old World Santa. Very rare, match holder with striker on back, made in red, brown, and green. Marked – see Fig. 134. $4800-5500.

Fig. 85. Spiny Shell. Pearlized finish with exceptional color, more common than most of the other figurals. Unmarked. $200-250.

Florals

Fig. 86. Tapestry. *Left)* Roses, large, pink. Unmarked. $200-300. *Right)* Roses, large pink and white. Unmarked. $250-350.

Fig. 87. *Left)* Rose Tapestry with Border Roses. Small pink roses form a border around the top of the holder. Unmarked. $350-500. *Right)* Rose Tapestry, assortment of roses cover the entire body of the holder. Unmarked. $350-450.

Fig. 88. Queen's Rose, hand painted, three handles. Marked – see Fig. 135, plus "Hand Painted Roses Her Majesty". $400-550.

Fig. 89. Blue rose on blue background, rare color. Marked – see Fig. 135. $350-450.

Fig. 90. Old Ivory decoration. *Left)* Glossy finish floral. Marked – see Fig. 135. $400-500. *Right)* Matte finish floral. Marked – see Fig. 135. $450-600.

Fig. 91. *Left)* Mums, rare decoration, three handles meet over the top of the holder, three feet that come part way up the body of the holder. Marked – see Fig. 135. $450-550. *Right)* Colonial Curtsy Scene. Four feet, two handles. Unmarked. $250-350.

Fig. 92. Floral. *Left)* Variety of floral designs found on this shape. Marked – V. $250-300. *Right)* Orchid, very rare floral. Marked – see Fig. 135. $350-400.

People and People with Animals

Fig. 93. Arabs. *Left)* Arab on brown horse carrying flag. Marked – #20 and #14. $250-300. *Right)* Three Arabs on horses. Marked – #26. $250-300.

Fig. 94. Arabs. *Left)* Arab on brown horse facing straight ahead, rare basket shape with three small V-shaped feet. Marked – see Fig. 135. $225-278. *Right)* One Arab on horseback and one on foot. Marked – #20. $250-300.

Fig. 95. Arabs. *Left)* Arab with camel. Marked – #46. $250-300. *Right)* Arab on white horse, very rare shape with beads at rim. Unmarked. $300-350.

Fig. 96. *Left)* The Fishermen. Two fishermen in boat, unusual "stub" handles. Marked – see Fig. 135. $350-400. *Right)* Lone Fisherman. Single fisherman standing in boat. Unmarked. $350-400.

Fig. 97. Hunter with Dog. *Left)* Gun at rest. Marked – see Fig. 135. $350-400. *Right)* Gun aimed. Marked – see Fig. 135. $300-350.

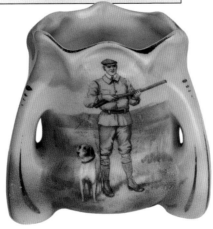

Fig. 98. The Hunt. *Left)* Lone horsewoman with hounds, unique shape with openwork at top. Marked – see Fig. 135. $300-350. *Right)* Lone horseman with hounds, kettle shape. Marked – see Fig. 135. $250-300.

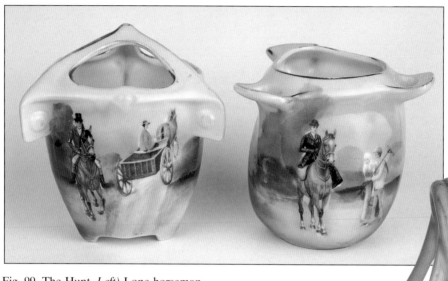

Fig. 99. The Hunt. *Left)* Lone horseman with woman and cart in background. Marked – see Fig. 135. $300-350. *Right)* Lone horsewoman with farm couple in background. Marked – see Fig. 135. $300-350.

Fig. 100. The Hunt. Double holder with twisted handle, two versions of the hunters with hounds. Marked – see Fig. 135. $300-375.

Fig. 101. Otter Hunter. *Left)* Standing with dogs, rare decoration, rare shape with crimped rim. Marked – see Fig. 135. $300-350. *Right)* Different scene, hunter bent over dogs. Unmarked. $300-350.

Fig. 102. Chicken Farmer. *Left)* Man feeding chickens. Unmarked. $200-250. *Right)* Lady feeding chickens, rare shape with tall loop handle. Unmarked. $250-300.

Fig. 103. Turkey Tender. *Left)* Three handles meet over top. Marked – #26 and #27. $250-300. *Right)* Unusual to see such detailed background. Marked – #37 and #40. $250-300.

Fig. 104. Sheep. *Left)* Two women tending sheep. Marked – see Fig. 135, #24. $200-250. *Right)* Different scene of two women tending sheep. Marked – #24 and #25. $200-250.

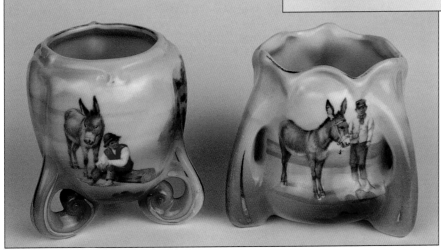

Fig. 105. Donkey with Boy. *Left)* Boy sitting on log, three heavy spiral feet. Unmarked. $250-350. *Right)* Boy standing. Marked – see Fig. 135. $250-350.

41

Fig. 106. Goose Girl. *Left)* Gold markings on feet, more scenic background. Marked – see Fig. 135, #10 and #17. $250-325. *Right)* Different background. Marked – see Fig. 135. $250-300.

Fig. 107. *Left)* Muff Lady. Tapestry. Unmarked. $350-400. *Right)* Goose Girl. Tapestry. Unmarked. $300-350.

Fig. 108. *Left)* Lady with Horse. Horse on left. Marked – see Fig. 135. $300-350. *Right)* Work Horse. Farm scene in background, also known without the farm scene, transfer on top half, bottom half painted bright orange. Marked – see Fig. 135. $250-300.

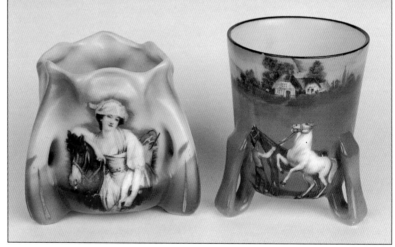

Fig. 109. *Left)* Lady with Horse. Horse on right. Unmarked. $300-350. *Right)* Cottage or Farm House. Winter scene, unusual pink band at top, hard to find shape. Unmarked. $250-350.

Fig. 110. Brittany Women. *Left)* Lifting two-handled basket. Marked – see Fig. 135. $250-350. *Right)* Fish basket around neck. Marked – see Fig. 135. $250-350.

Fig. 111. Brittany Women. *Left)* Lifting two-handled basket, typical background. Marked – see Fig. 135. $250-350. *Right)* Same transfer, but totally different background than usually shown with Brittany Women, sailboat in background. Unmarked. $300-375.

Fig. 112. Gleaners. *Left)* Harvesting wheat. Marked – #32. $250-300. *Right)* Different scene with scythe. Unmarked. $250-300.

Fig. 113. *Left)* Horse and Carriage. Unmarked. $300-350. *Right)* Peasant Ladies with sheep. Unmarked. $250-300.

Fig. 114. *Left)* Colonial Couple. Walking with dog. Signed "Gainsborough." Marked – see Fig. 135. $300-350. *Right)* Courting Couple. Playing mandolin. Unmarked. $300-350.

Fig. 115. *Left)* Prince and His Lady. Four feet, two handles. Marked – see Fig. 135. $300-350. *Right)* Colonial Curtsy Scene. Three feet, handles that meet over the top of the holder. Marked – see Fig. 135. $300-350.

Fig. 116. Peering Lady. *Left)* Glossy finish. Marked – see Fig. 135. $300-350. *Right)* Tapestry. Unmarked. $300-375.

Fig. 117. Shawl Lady. *Left)* Tapestry. Unmarked. $350-450. *Right)* Same. Unmarked. $350-450.

Fig. 118. *Left)* The Messenger. Marked – see Fig. 131. $375-400. *Right)* Lawyer. Rare decoration. Note detail in picture – quill on desk, file cabinet, drawer on floor, papers, room divider. Unmarked. $400-450.

Fig. 119. Peasant Musicians. *Left)* Playing fiddle and clarinet, rare shape. Marked – see Fig. 135. $300-375. *Right)* Playing cello and mandolin. Marked – see Fig. 135. $250-300.

Fig. 120. *Left)* Cavalier Musicians with Mandolin. Marked – see Fig. 135. $375-450. *Right)* The "Toaster" Cavalier. Marked – see Fig. 135. $400-450.

Fig. 121. *Left)* Castle by the Lake. Tapestry. Unmarked. $400-450. *Right)* The "Toaster" Cavalier. Tapestry. Marked – see Fig. 135. $400-450.

Fig. 122. Scenic tapestry. Unmarked. $250-300.

Miscellaneous

Fig. 123. Blue Onion. *Left)* Also known as Old Tettau Blue, old Royal Tettau mark, one of their first patterns. Marked – capital "T" with a period. $150-200. *Right)* Same pattern, but could have been made by Royal Copenhagen or another manufacturer. Unmarked. $65-95.

Fig. 124. Sailboat. Very rare decoration and color. Marked – see Fig. 131. $300-350.

Fig. 125. Children Playing. Steamboat in background. Unmarked. $300-400.

Fig. 126. Corinthian (or Classic). *Left)* Typical black background with orange inner rim, figure facing left. Marked – see Fig. 135. $200-250. *Right)* Figure facing right, rare shape with single loop handle extending above top rim, unusual in that it does not have the orange inner rim. Marked – see Fig. 135. $250-300.

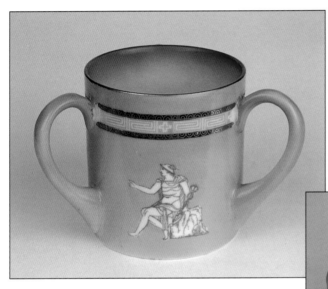

Fig. 127. Corinthian (or Classic). Rare green background with orange inner rim, three handles, figure facing left. Corinthian can also be found with a red background and a yellow background. Marked – see Fig. 135 plus "Corinthian Ware." $250-350.

Fig. 128. Jester. *Left)* Rare shape with crimped rim, three handles. "A Kindly Word Cools Anger." Signed "Noke." Unmarked. $500-700. *Right)* "Welcome is the Best Cheer." Signed "Noke." Unmarked. $500-700.

Fig. 129. Sunset. *Left)* Boat in background. Marked – see Fig. 135. $350-400. *Right)* Reverse view. Marked – see Fig. 135. $350-400.

Fig. 130. Sunset, rare with blue coloring instead of the more common orange. May be small vase. Unmarked. $350-450.

Royal Bayreuth Marks

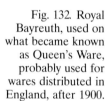

Fig. 131. Royal Bayreuth, "green mark," used for wares exported to England, c. 1919.

Fig. 132. Royal Bayreuth, used on what became known as Queen's Ware, probably used for wares distributed in England, after 1900.

Fig. 133. Royal Bayreuth, common "blue mark" plus an importer's mark for Burley & Tyrrell Co., Chicago, IL (1871-1919), dates for mark are unknown.

Fig. 134. Royal Bayreuth, used for wares exported to United States, c. 1919.

Fig. 135. Royal Bayreuth, common "blue mark," used for wares exported to the United States after 1900.

Fig. 136. Gobelin Ware in circle with sun. Example of a customer's mark used by Royal Bayreuth when producing wares for that customer. No date given.

Czechoslovakia

Toothpicks marked Czechoslovakia would have been produced after 1918, when the area was officially named Czechoslovakia. Prior to that time, wares made in these same factories would have been marked Austria. In fact, some factories are known to have continued to use a backstamp showing Austria as the country of origin after 1918.

This area is the home of Count Thun's Porcelain Factory (1819-1945) which produced the popular line of porcelains labeled Vienna. Bohemian ware was very popular in the United States and much of it was imported by P. H. Leonard and later by Bawo & Dotter. Both decorated and undecorated wares were brought into the United States. The importer's backstamp is sometimes found in place of that of the factory.

As with other areas known for the production of fine porcelain, the Bohemian factories thrived because of the rich natural resources in the area. The porcelains that were produced were of an excellent quality and remain in great demand.

Fig. 137. *Left)* Marked – crown, "T K Czechoslovakia" c. 1918-1939. Artist signed "M. B. Hatch." $35-45. *Right)* Three handles. Marked – crown, "T K Czechoslovakia" c. 1918-1939. Artist initials "FN." Note: This is a Schlegelmilch mold also found marked RS Prussia and RS Germany. $30-40.

Fig. 138. *Left)* Five handles. Marked – Czechoslovakia. $35-45. *Right)* Unmarked. Sometimes found marked Czechoslovakia. $30-35.

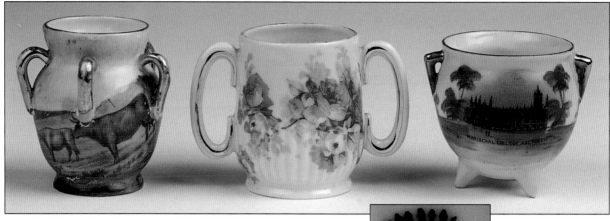

Fig. 139. *Left)* Five handles. Marked – see Fig. 140. $35-45. *Center)* Marked – see Fig. 140. $35-45. *Right)* Three feet, two handle. Marked – see Fig. 140. $35-45.

Fig. 141. Playing cards, different on each side. Marked – see Fig. 142. $35-45.

Fig. 140. Schmidt & Co. Bohemia (Czechoslovakia), c. 1904-1945.

Fig. 142. United Porcelain Factory Klosterle, Czechoslovakia, c. 1921-1927.

Fig. 143. Card scene, sometimes marked Czechoslovakia. Marked – Mustershutz. $30-40.

England

The Victorian era was the heyday for the toothpick holder. With their close association to England, Americans loved anything that might be associated with the Queen. So the question arises, did Queen Victoria have a toothpick holder on her table? If anyone knows for sure, it would be an interesting fact to document.

We know that very few toothpicks were produced in England, though many of the famous Royal Doulton pieces originally made as vases have been adopted as toothpicks. Most English holders are of soft paste porcelain. They tend to be plainer mold designs and are decorated with transfers more often then being hand painted.

Fig. 144. *Left)* Mosaic design. Marked – Wedgwood. $50-65. *Center)* Pedestal. Marked – see Fig. 171. $40-50. *Right)* Inside Rim has floral transfer. Marked – see Fig. 172. $50-65.

Fig. 145. Spode. Marked – see Fig. 172. $50-65.

Fig. 146. Wedgwood Lustre. Known to collectors as Fairyland Lustre, designed by Susannah Margaretta "Daisy" Makeig-Jones, 1914-1931, only one toothpick shape known. *Left)* Butterfly, three handles. $375-425. *Right)* Exotic bird, three handles. $375-425.

Fig. 147. Wedgwood Lustre. *Left)* Dragon and snake, three handles. $375-425. *Right)* Swallows, three handles. $375-425.

Fig. 148. Wedgwood Lustre. *Left)* Butterfly, three handles. $375-425.
Right) Fruit, three handles. $375-425.

Fig. 149. Wedgwood
Lustre. Interior of
Butterfly decoration.

Fig. 150. Aynsley. Marked – see Fig. 174.
$40-50.

Fig. 151. *Left)* Five handles, sometimes marked Victoria, England. Unmarked. $30-40. *Center)* Gold lined interior. Marked – see Fig. 174. $50-60.
Right) Floral chintz. Marked – Royal Winton. $50-60.

Fig. 152. *Left)* Possibly Aynsley. Unmarked. $50-60. *Right)* Three feet. Unmarked. $30-35.

Fig. 153. Royal Crown Derby. Beautiful gold scrolling around rim. Marked – see Fig. 175. $85-95.

Fig. 154. Royal Crown Derby. *Left)* Three handles, floral. Marked – see Fig. 175. $85-95. *Right)* Three handles, ornate design. Marked – see Fig. 175. $100-150.

Fig. 155. Royal Crown Derby. Heavy gold and cobalt. Unmarked. $275-350.

Fig. 156. *Left)* Thistle shape mold. Marked – Hammersley, crown. $45-55. *Right)* Dresden. Vegetable shaped mold. Marked – see Fig. 176. $35-45.

Fig. 157. *Left)* Hexagon shaped. Marked – Delphine China, Made in England. $35-45. *Center)* Marked – Turnivals, Made in England. $30-40. *Right)* Marked – Coalport. $60-75.

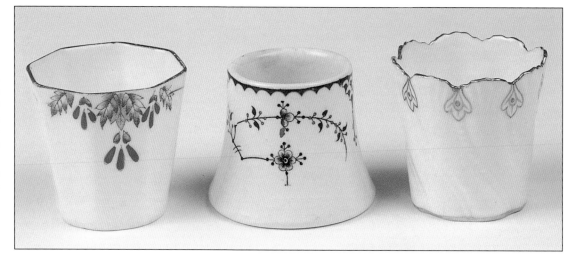

Fig. 158. Shelley China. Marked – shield, Shelley Fine Bone China, England. $35-45.

Fig. 159. Crown Straffordshire. Marked – see Fig. 177. $55-65.

Fig. 160. Royal Worcester. *Left)* Marked – see Fig. 178. $75-85. *Right)* Marked – see Fig. 178. $85-110.

Fig. 161. Royal Worcester. Marked – Royal Worcester, Made in England. $75-90.

Fig. 162. Royal Worcester. Marked – crown & circle. Royal Worcester Porcelain Company, England, c. 1890. $85-120.

Fig. 163. Royal Worcester. Marked – see Fig. 178. $50-65.

Fig. 164. Marked – BCM Nelsonware,
Made in England. $45-50.

Fig. 165. Jasperware. Marked –
Adams, England. $50-75.

Fig. 166. *Left)* Marked – Duson Hanley, England. $35-45.
Right) Three handles, crested "Glasgow" Unmarked. $35-45.

Fig. 167. Jasperware. Marked –
Dudson Hanley, England. $40-50.

Fig. 168. *Left)* Three handles, Goss type. Unmarked. $35-45. *Center)* Goss. Marked – WH Goss, bird. $35-45. *Right)* Goss type. Unmarked. $35-45.

Fig. 169. *Left)* Goss type. Marked – Arcadia China. $35-45.
Center) Goss type. Marked – Derwent China. $35-45.
Right) Goss. Marked – WH Goss, bird. $35-45.

Fig. 170. *Left)* Goss. Marked – WH Goss. $35-45. *Right)* Three handles. Marked – Arcadia China. $35-45.

Fig. 172. Copeland Spode England mark. Copeland & Sons, Stoke, England, c. 1920.

Fig. 171. Hammersley & Co., c. 1887-present.

Fig. 173. Wedgwood. Lustre ware produced between 1914-1931.

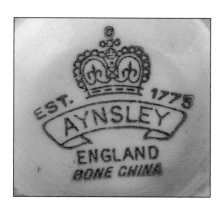

Fig. 174. John Aynsley & Sons, Staffordshire, England, c. 1891-present.

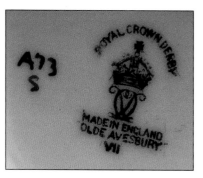

Fig. 175. Derby Porcelain Works, Derby, England, c. 1890-1940.

Fig. 176. Dresden, England. No information found.

Fig. 177. Crown Staffordshire Porcelain Company, Fenton, England, c. 1906-1930.

Fig. 178. Worcester Royal Porcelain Company, c. 1890.

Royal Doulton

Most of the toothpicks we know and collect as Royal Doulton were produced by Doulton and Company, founded in 1853. However, the history of the Doulton family and their various porcelain factories goes back to the early 1800s. Most famous for their character jugs and figurines, they actually produced a wide range of porcelain items. Charles Noke worked with them as a designer and was probably the one responsible for the development of their series wares, the most popular of which is the Dickens Ware series.

Nearly all Doulton toothpicks are marked with a backstamp, most of which feature a lion standing on a crown. The words Royal Doulton were first used on the marks in 1902 and "Made in England" was added after 1930. Some backstamps used are specific to the series or type of ware on which they are found.

Some of the Doulton toothpicks may have originally been intended as small vases or match holders. While any Royal Doulton toothpicks are hard to find, the series ware seem to be the most readily available and the most popular. The character toothpicks and the Santa Claus pattern are the rarest. This section will show representative examples of the various toothpick shapes and of the various patterns.

Fig. 179. Royal Doulton. Sairey Gamp (1940-1942) – from *Martin Chuzzlewit* by Charles Dickens, one of five known toby-like character toothpick holders, all very hard to find. Others are Fat Boy – from *The Pickwick Papers* by Charles Dickens; Old Charlie (1940-1969) – a 19th century watchman; Paddy (1940-1941) – an Irishman and The Falconer – trainer of birds. Marked – see Fig. 198. $375-500.

Fig. 180. Royal Doulton. Dickens Ware Series. *Left)* Sam Weller. Marked – see Fig. 198. $95-120. *Center)* Mr. Micawber. Marked – see Fig. 198. $95-120. *Right)* Mr. Pickwick. Marked – see Fig. 198. $95-120.

Fig. 182. Royal Doulton. *Left)* Robin Hood. "Little John and Alan A Dale." Marked – see Fig. 195. $95-120. *Right)* Golfers. Different image on each side. Marked – see Fig. 198. $95-110.

Fig. 181. Royal Doulton. Dickens Ware Series. Mr. Micawber. Marked – see Fig. 199. $145-160.

Fig. 183. Royal Doulton. *Left)* Cottage with sheep. Large size with irregular top. Marked – see Fig. 198. $100-125. *Right)* Dickens Series, Orlando. Common shape. Marked – see Fig. 198. $95-100.

Fig. 184. Royal Doulton. *Left)* Welsh Ladies. Side view of ladies, rare shape. Marked – see Fig. 198. $95-120. *Right)* Jody Weller. Marked – see Fig. 198. $120-150.

Fig. 185. Royal Doulton. *Left)* Welsh Ladies. Two ladies walking. Marked – see Fig. 198. $100-145. *Right)* Welsh Ladies. Group of four ladies. Marked – see Fig. 198. $100-145.

Fig. 186. Royal Doulton. *Left)* Santa Claus. Very rare decoration, unusual shape. "Tobacco and a good coal fire are things this season doth require." Marked – see Fig. 198. $300-350. *Right)* Pilgrims. Marked – see Fig. 196. $125-160.

Fig. 187. Royal Doulton. *Left)* Isacc Walton Series. Fishing, different image on each side, green tree background. Signed "Noke," a popular artist who worked with multiple porcelain manufacturers, his signature is also seen on Japanese items and Royal Bayreuth. Marked – see Fig. 198. $95-120. *Right)* Isaac Walton. Fishing, different images than shown on the other example, black tree background. Signed "Noke." Marked – see Fig. 194. $95-120.

Fig. 188. Royal Doulton. *Left)* Two handles. Marked – see Fig. 198. $95-120. *Right)* Two handles. Marked – see Fig. 198. $100-130.

Fig. 189. Royal Doulton. *Left)* Horse and Riders. Square shape, trees on back. Marked – see Fig. 198. $95-100. *Right)* Carriage Scene. Square shape, trees on back. Marked – see Fig. 198. $95-100.

Fig. 190. Royal Doulton. *Left)* Costumes. Different image of one, two, or three people on each side. Marked – see Fig. 198. $80-100. *Right)* Tam O'Shanter. Inn scene with table and pitchers, sterling rim. On back, "Kings may be blast, but Tam was glorious. Oe'r a the ills o' life victorious. Burns." Marked – see Fig. 197. $80-100.

Fig. 191. Royal Doulton. *Left)* Hoo-poe Bird (several different spellings used). Floral decoration at top. Marked – see Fig. 198. $75-100. *Right)* Couples. One or two people on each side, each side different. Marked – see Fig. 198. $75-95.

Fig. 192. Royal Doulton. *Left)* Geese and Holly Leaves. Harder to find shape. Marked – see Fig. 198. $95-120. *Right)* Floral. Hand painted, unusual shape. Marked – see Fig. 198. $80-95.

Fig. 193. Royal Doulton. *Left)* Floral, simple design. Marked – see Fig. 198. $75-95. *Right)* Floral, simple design. Marked – see Fig. 198. $75-95.

France

Most French porcelain comes from the Limoges area of France where kaolin clay is abundant. With this type of clay readily available, numerous factories, including the famed Haviland factory, produced some of the finest, purest porcelain in the world. In the latter part of the nineteenth century, the most talented artists in Europe migrated to France to practice their art on this fine porcelain. As a result of this, you will find many beautiful, hand painted pieces.

Fig. 194. Royal Doulton, Isaac Walton series, c. 1906-1930s.

Fig. 195. Royal Doulton, Under the Greenwood Tree series, c. 1909.

Fig. 196. Royal Doulton, green, c. 1902-1922, 1927-1932.

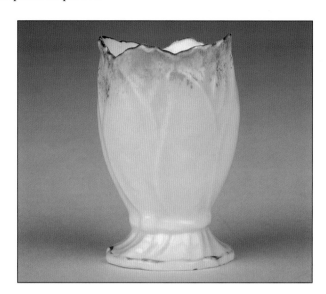

Fig. 200. Marked – Limoges, France. $45-65

Fig. 197. Royal Doulton, red, c. 1902-1922, 1927-1932.

Fig. 201. Hand painted, inside pearlized. Marked – see Fig. 202. $45-60.

Fig. 198. Royal Doulton, c. 1901-1930s. "Made in England" added just above the words "Royal Doulton" in the 1930s.

Fig. 199. Royal Doulton, Burslem, Staffordshire, England, c. 1922.

Fig. 202. J P L France mark. La Ceramiqe, Jean Pouyat Limoges, France, c. 1905.

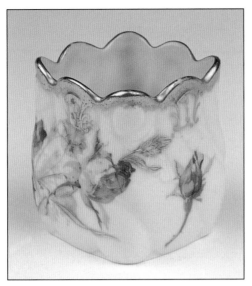

Fig. 203. Square, hand painted.
Marked – crown and "Coronet"
underneath, Limoges. $45-60.

Fig. 204. Luster inside. Marked – B & C
Limoges, France. $45-60.

Fig. 205. *Left)* Hand painted egg shape. Marked – France. $35-45.
Right) Hand painted pedestal. Marked – Giraud, Limoges. $35-45.

Fig. 207. Guerin-
Pouyat-Elite
Porcelain Factory
LTD. c. 1900.

Fig. 206. *Left)* Hand painted. Marked – P L Limoges, France. $35-
45. *Right)* Hand painted. Marked – BM Elite, see Fig. 207. $50-70.

64

Fig. 208. Interesting silver overlay and attached plate. Three different backstamps, the manufacturer, decorator, and importer. Marked – H&C France, Haviland & Co., Banks & Biddles. $50-65.

Fig. 209. Marked – B&C France. $50-65.

Fig. 210. Hand painted. Marked – France. $50-65.

Fig. 211. *Left)* Hand painted floral. Marked – see Fig. 212. $35-45. *Center)* Marked – Limoges, France. $35-45. *Right)* Floral with gold bands. Marked – PL over Limoges. $35-45.

Fig. 212. Guerin-Pouyet-Elite, Limoges, France, c. 1901.

65

Germany

Germany was one of the main exporters of porcelain toothpick holders. Besides the well-known Schlegelmilch-related factories located in Prussia, there were numerous other manufacturers. The quality of the porcelain and the designs can vary dramatically. More translucent, lightweight porcelain holders usually have a more defined mold design and are glazed on the bottom. Often, they are hand decorated and the designs are quite ornate and detailed. Heavier, lesser quality pieces tend to have imperfections in the porcelain and an unglazed bottom. The decorations may be less ornate and the porcelain itself may be an off color. Many German toothpicks were not marked, making identifying the manufacturer and tracing the history very difficult.

To complicate research even more, we have discovered a number of toothpick shapes marked Germany that can also be found with a mark from Austria or Czechoslovakia, both of which were under the German Empire at various times in history. There may have been German-related factories in those areas or the molds may have been made in Germany and then sold to other factories which did the decorating and then applied their own mark. We have tried to indicate when a mold has contradictory marks.

During the Gilded Era, china painting was a popular hobby, especially for Victorian ladies. For the most part, German porcelain factories were the suppliers of items for this favorite pastime. The plain white, glazed porcelain items were referred to as "blanks." You will find many blanks that were hand painted and often signed by the artist. This type of painting is easily identified, as it is often a sweet floral motif. Though some are very well done, many can be identified as the work of a novice painter. They are to be admired for the time, patience, and love that went into creating them.

Also at that time, there were many American art studios that received the blanks. They employed incredibly talented artists who produced some of the most amazing pieces, making hand painted china a much sought after collectible. You will find these hand painted holders shown in among the factory decorated ones since we have organized the photographs by country of origin and manufacturer.

We have separated the marked German toothpicks from the unmarked to make it easier for you to associate the various marks with the toothpicks. Unmarked toothpicks will be included in a separate section that follows the manufacturer's marks.

Note: Toothpicks marked R. S. Germany or known to be R. S. Germany are included in the Prussia section since they are more closely related to the Prussian manufacturers.

Fig. 213. Wonderful hand painting. Marked – Dresden, crown over "H". $70-80.

Fig. 214. Romance scene. Marked – RK Dresden Germany. Richard Klemm, c. 1886-1916. $75-90.

Fig. 215. *Left)* C&E Carsten. Dogwood blossom. Marked – see Fig. 235. $35-45. *Center)* Hand painted heavier weight porcelain mold that was originally made in a pattern glass toothpick, Vermont by US Glass Company. Marked – Germany. $40-50. *Right)* Dresden. Floral. Marked – see Fig. 236. $65-80.

Fig. 216. *Left)* Square. Marked – Germany in script. $25-35. *Center)* Floral. Marked – see Fig. 235. $35-45. *Right)* Tapered floral. Marked – in script Olimpic, Germany. $25-35.

Fig. 217. C&E Carsten. *Left)* Marked – see Fig. 235. $30-40. *Center)* Marked – see Fig. 235. $30-40. *Right)* Marked – see Fig. 235. $30-40.

Fig. 218*. Left)* C&E Carsten. Hexagon shaped. Marked – see Fig. 235. $40-50. *Center)* Marked – see Fig. 237. $40-50. *Right)* Highly embossed flowers. Unmarked. $40-50.

Fig. 219. C&E Carsten. *Left)* Marked – see Fig. 235. $30-40. *Center)* Unmarked. $30-40. *Right)* Marked – see Fig. 235. $35-45.

Fig. 220*. Left)* Yellow roses. Marked – Germany in red. $30-40. *Right)* Pink roses. Marked – Germany in green. $30-40.

Fig. 221. *Left)* Marked – Germany. $35-45. *Center)* Marked –
Germany. $30-40. *Right)* Luster top. Marked – Germany. $35-45.

Fig. 222. *Left)* Rose with lustre. Marked – see Fig. 237. $40-50.
Center) Floral, Prussia related mold. Marked – Germany. $40-50.
Right) Marked – Made in Germany. $35-45.

Fig. 223. *Left)* Beautifully detailed decoration. Marked – see Fig. 238. $50-60. *Center)* Hand
painted. Unmarked. $40-50. *Right)* Hand painted. Marked – HC Royal, crown & shield. $35-45.

Fig. 224. *Left)* Pink roses. Marked – see Fig. 239. $40-50. *Center)* Prussia mold 525. Unmarked. $75-100. *Right)* Pink rose. Marked – E & R Germany. $40-50.

Fig. 225. Two unusual handles. Marked – Germany. $35-45.

Fig. 226. *Left)* Unusual shape with cherry. Marked – Made in Germany. $35-45.
Right) Three Crown China. Pink cascades of roses. Marked – see Fig. 243. $40-50.

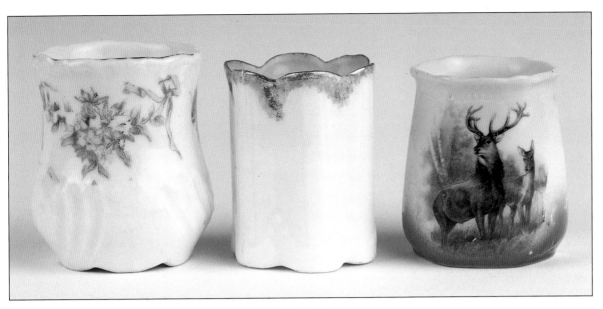

Fig. 227. *Left)* Floral. Unmarked. $30-40. *Center)* Prussia mold, pink blush inside rim. Marked – see Fig. 440. $40-60. *Right)* Three Crown China. Deer scene. Marked – see Fig. 243. $45-55.

Fig. 228. *Left)* Krister Porcelain. Art Deco design. Marked – see Fig. 240. $35-45. *Right)* Three Crown China. Pink roses. Marked – see Fig. 243. $35-45.

Fig. 229. Krister Porcelain. Condiment set, pink floral w/ heavy gold; salt, pepper, two handle toothpick on tray. Marked – see Fig. 240. $65-85 for the set.

Fig. 230. Swaine & Co. German Delft. This style shown with three different marks. See Fig. 241. $50-65 each.

Silesia

Silesia is another of those areas that was under the rule of different countries at different times. It was a part of Prussia up until 1871 when the German Empire was formed. At that time, it became a part of the Prussian Kingdom within the German Empire. Later, in 1945 with the defeat of the German Reich, it became a part of Poland. Because of all of these changes, it can be difficult to determine the age of toothpicks from Silesia. Those marked Silesia could have been produced anytime between 1882 and 1918. They were marked Prussia only between the years 1902 and 1918, and Germany was used from 1882 and 1928. The majority of the toothpicks are marked Silesia, and a few are marked Germany.

There were more than twenty porcelain factories operating in Silesia, but perhaps the best known is that of Hermann Ohme, the Porcelain Manufactory Hermann Ohme, which was in production from 1881 to 1929. They produced an extensive line of china, much of which was exported to the United States.

Ohme produced the very popular Old Ivory designs, characterized by their creamy, white background and various borders done in brown and gold. The background and borders were hand painted, but the primary decoration was done by various artist-designed decals. Typically, the decals were touched up by hand after they were applied. Floral patterns are the most common, and holly patterns are one of the most sought after – and there is a holly toothpick. Old Ivory toothpicks are known in three different molds: Clairon,

Eglantine, and Carmen. Toothpicks with other Ohme decorations are also know in Elysee, Florette, and Quadrille molds.

The Ohme mark is rather unique and difficult to describe. It is a bit like a fleur-de-lis created with a stylized "O" near the top and a stylized "H" at the bottom. A crown sits above. Items may also be marked with the name of the mold and/or a number that identifies the pattern.

Naturally, with the popularity of Old Ivory, the designs were bound to be copied. Many factories were eager for a portion of the lucrative export trade. One of the largest competitors was Three Crown China, and you will find a number of toothpicks made by them. Three Crown China (1881-1953) produced many items similar to those offered by Ohme, but they are of lesser quality china and the decoration is not as well done.

Fig. 231. Silesia. *Left)* Transfer decoration. Marked – O H (Hermann Ohme) symbol, Silesia. $65-85. *Center)* Hand painted, artist signed, "McB". Also found with the Old Ivory decoration. $55-70. *Right)* Highly detailed Eglantine mold, found with a wide variety of decorations. Marked – see Fig. 242. $50-70.

Fig. 232. Three Crown China. *Left)* Water lily. Marked – see Fig. 243.
$40-55. *Right)* Pink Rose. Marked – see Fig. 243. $40-55.

Fig. 233. Three Crown China, 1881-1953. Decorated in the style of Old Ivory produced by Hermann Ohme, an obvious attempt at capitalizing on the popularity of the Old Ivory line. Most popular design has a shamrock border. Design detail is good, but the quality of the china is inferior to the Ohme product. *Left)* Marked – see Fig. 243. $60-80. *Right)* Marked – see Fig. 243. $60-80.

Fig. 234. Old Ivory. Fine quality china produced by the Hermann Ohme factory. Toothpicks in the Holly pattern are very rare. *Left)* Carmen mold, pattern #84. Marked – see Fig. 244. $200-300. *Center)* Clairon mold, pattern #16. Marked – see Fig. 244. $200-300. *Right)* Eglantine mold, pattern #84. Marked – see Fig. 244. $200-300.

German Marks

Fig. 235. C&E Carsten Porcelain Factory, Thuringia, c. 1918.

Fig. 236. Dresden, Made in Germany. No additional information found.

Fig. 237. Possibly Kampfe & List Porcelain Factory, Germany.

Fig. 238. Prussia related.

Fig. 239. Germany. No information found.

Fig. 240. Krister Porcelain Manufacturer, Silesia, Germany, c. 1904-1927.

Fig. 241. All are Swaine & Co. Germany, c. 1900-1920.

Fig. 242. Hermann Ohme, stylized O H in a fleur-de-lis type design. *Left)* c. 1882-1918. *Right)* c. 1882-1921.

Fig. 243. Three Crown China, c. 1881-1953.

Fig. 244. Hermann Ohme, Old Ivory, stylized O H in a fleur-de-lis type design, plus Old Ivory, c. 1882-1918.

Unmarked

The toothpicks shown in this section are either unmarked or simply marked "Germany." Two categories included in this section are Carnival Lustre and Elfinware. Both types of china were made in Germany and have unique details worth mentioning.

Fig. 245. *Left)* Floral. Unmarked. $35-45. *Center)* Hand painted dots. Unmarked. $20-25. *Right)* Hand painted floral. Unmarked. $25-35.

Fig. 246. *Left)* Unmarked. $35-45. *Center)* Unmarked. $35-45. *Right)* Unmarked. $35-45.

Fig. 247. *Left)* Avocado shaped. Unmarked. $20-25. *Center)* Cobalt with boys face. Unmarked. $20-30. *Right)* Leaf design. Unmarked. $20-30.

Fig. 248. *Left)* Bulbous floral. Unmarked. $35-45. *Center)* Bell flowers. Marked – raised bar. $20-35. *Right)* Pink flowers, Prussia mold 10. Unmarked. $50-75.

Fig. 249. *Left)* Hand painted. Unmarked. $25-35. *Right)* Hand painted. Unmarked. $25-35.

Fig. 250. *Left)* Leaf design in mold. Unmarked. $15-25. *Center)* Lobed base. Unmarked. $20-30. *Right)* Pleated base. Unmarked. $25-35.

Fig. 251. *Left)* Possibly German. Unmarked. $20-30. *Center)* Pretty embossing. Unmarked. $35-45. *Right)* Possibly German. Unmarked. $20-30.

Fig. 252. *Left)* Embossed braid around rim. Unmarked. $20-30.
Right) Embossed flowers, hand painted. Unmarked. $20-30.

Fig. 253. *Left)* Unmarked. $20-30. *Center)*
Unmarked. $20-30. *Right)* Unmarked. $20-30.

Fig. 254. *Left)* Thin porcelain, exquisitely done. Unmarked. $35-50. *Center)* Thin porcelain. Unmarked. $30-40. *Right)* Unmarked. $25-35.

Fig. 255. *Left)* Unmarked. $30-40. *Center)* Lustre finish. Unmarked. $20-30. *Right)* Mold detail around base. Unmarked. $20-30.

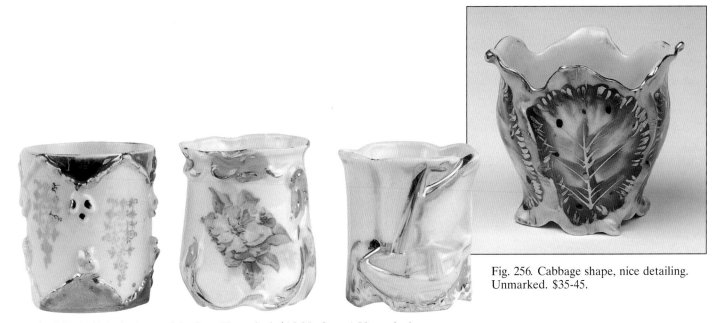

Fig. 256. Cabbage shape, nice detailing. Unmarked. $35-45.

Fig. 257. *Left)* Raised porcelain dots. Unmarked. $15-25. *Center)* Unmarked. $30-40. *Right)* Raised boat shape in mold. Unmarked. $20-30.

Fig. 258. *Left)* Unmarked. $35-45. *Center)* Peach with floral. Unmarked. $20-30. *Right)* Mold often found as match with striker. Unmarked. $20-30.

Fig. 259. *Left)* Hand painted floral. Unmarked. $20-30. *Right)* Hand painted, monogrammed. Unmarked. $35-50.

Fig. 260. *Left)* Unmarked. $20-30. *Center)* Attractive mold design. Unmarked. $30-40. *Right)* Unmarked. $20-30.

Fig. 261. *Left)* Unmarked. $20-30. *Center)* Unmarked. $25-35. *Right)* Gathered rim. Unmarked. $25-35.

Fig. 262. *Left)* Pedestal. Unmarked. $25-35. *Center)* Hexagon, flow blue. Unmarked. $25-35. *Right)* Orange flowers, early Prussia mold 75. Unmarked. $35-50.

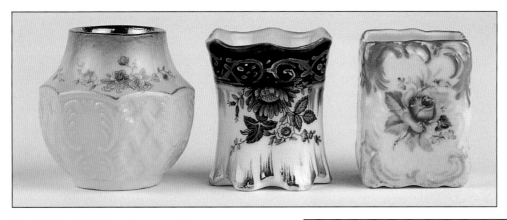

Fig. 263. *Left)* Embossed unusual shape. Unmarked. $25-35. *Center)* Flow blue with beautiful gold detail, thin porcelain. Unmarked. $35-45. *Right)* Square, thin porcelain, heavy gold detail. Unmarked. $30-40.

Fig. 264. *Left)* Unmarked. $25-35. *Right)* Unmarked. $25-35.

Fig. 265. *Left)* Unmarked. $35-50. *Center)* Unmarked. $35-45. *Right)* Unmarked. $35-45.

Fig. 266. *Left)* Unusual pierced front. Unmarked. $25-35. *Center)* Ruffled rim. Unmarked. $25-35. *Right)* Unmarked. $20-30.

Fig. 267. *Left)* Thin porcelain, fine ruffled top. Unmarked. $40-60. *Center)* Square, four feet. Unmarked. $40-60. *Right)* Thin porcelain, delicate fluted shaped mold with four feet. Unmarked. $40-60.

Fig. 268. *Left)* Prussia mold 343. Unmarked. $75-100. *Center)* Possibly early Prussia. Unmarked. $50-60. *Right)* Possibly early Prussia. Unmarked. $45-60.

Fig. 269. *Left)* Prussia mold 75. Unmarked. $40-60. *Center)* Unmarked. $20-30 *Right)* Unmarked. $20-30.

Fig. 270. *Left)* Unmarked. $35-45. *Center)* Hand painted floral. Unmarked. $25-50. *Right)* Hand painted roses. Unmarked. $30-40.

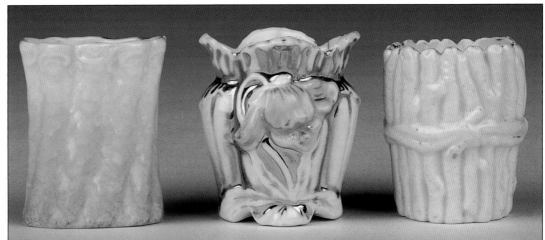

Fig. 271. *Left)* Unmarked. $20-30. *Center)* Highly embossed mold. Unmarked. $35-45. *Right)* Unmarked. $15-25.

Fig. 272. *Left)* Embossed rose in mold. Unmarked. $30-40. *Right)* Applied flowers and branches. Unmarked. $30-40.

Fig. 273. *Left)* Unmarked. $20-30. *Center)* Applied flowers. Unmarked. $20-30. *Right)* Applied details. Unmarked. $20-30.

Fig. 274. *Left)* Embossed. Unmarked. $20-30. *Center)* Embossed Lily of the Valley. Unmarked. $20-30. *Right)* Embossed sprig. Unmarked. $20-30.

Fig. 275. *Left)* Embossed pink lustre. Unmarked. $25-35. *Center)* Embossed pink lustre. Unmarked. $25-35. *Right)* Embossed pink lustre. Unmarked. $25-35.

Fig. 276. *Left)* Unique hand painted portrait. Unmarked. $35-45. *Center)* Hand painted. Unmarked. $45-50. *Right)* Paneled mold, four feet. Unmarked. $25-35.

Fig. 277. *Left)* Hand painted. Unmarked. $30-40. *Center)* Unmarked. $35-45. *Right)* Unmarked. $25-35.

Fig. 278. *Left)* Lady's portrait, possibly Prussia related. Unmarked. $30-50. *Right)* Lady's portrait, possibly Prussia related. Unmarked. $30-50.

Fig. 279. *Left)* Portrait of "Queen Louise." Unmarked. $40-50. *Right)* Portrait of "Girl with Daisy Crown." Unmarked. $30-40. Both transfers are Prussia-related.

Fig. 280. Made in Germany to imitate Wedgwood's famous Jasperware. The quality is not the same, but all types of this ware are coined Jasperware. *Left)* Unmarked. $25-35. *Center)* Marked – Made in Germany. $25-35 *Right)* Unmarked. $25-35.

Fig. 281. *Left)* Bisque, cupid. Unmarked. $20-30. *Right)* Bisque, leaf mold. Unmarked. $20-30.

Fig. 282. *Left)* Raised porcelain dots, embossed flowers and leaves. Unmarked. $35-45. *Center)* Hunt scene. Unmarked. $30-40. *Right)* Raised porcelain dots. Unmarked. $25-35.

Fig. 283. Molds are Prussia related. *Left)* Deer scene transfers touched up with hand painting. Unmarked. $40-60. *Right)* Deer scene transfers touched up with hand painting. Unmarked. $40-60.

Fig. 284. *Left)* Unmarked. $25-35. *Center)* Swan scene. Unmarked. $35-45. *Right)* Embossed top. Unmarked. $25-35.

Fig. 285. *Left)* Hand painted, RSP mold OM140. Unmarked. $50-60. *Center)* Romance scene, Prussia related. Unmarked. $45-60. *Right)* Four feet, cobalt rim. Unmarked. $35-45.

Carnival Lustre

Carnival Lustre is a name we have applied to a unique type of German ware that has porcelain filigree, swags, beads, ropes, and other decorations applied to the blank prior to firing. They were then painted and a lustre finish applied to all or a portion of the body. Most are deco-rated with a lot of gold. They are very creative and have almost a "Mardi Gras" look to them. Most are simply marked "Germany," leaving us unable to identify the manufacturer.

Fig. 286. *Left)* Cranberry with applied flower. Unmarked. $25-35. *Right)* Waffle pattern. Unmarked. $20-30.

Fig. 287. *Left)* Yellow/purple lustre. Unmarked. $25-35. *Right)* Yellow/red lustre. Unmarked. $25-35.

Fig. 288. *Left)* Purple lustre. Un-marked. $25-35. *Center)* Cranberry lustre. Unmarked. $20-30. *Right)* Cranberry lustre. Unmarked. $25-35.

Fig. 289. *Left)* Green Lustre. Unmarked. $20-30. *Center)* Three handles. This is a Prussia related mold. Marked – Made in Germany. $35-45. *Right)* Yellow lustre. Unmarked. $25-35.

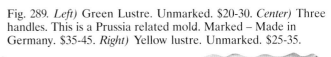

Fig. 290. Pink and yellow lustre. Unmarked. $30-40.

Fig. 291. Pedestal, nice applied decoration. Has four small feet under base. Unmarked. $25-35.

Elfinware

Elfinware is a whimsical collectible all on its own. The items are small porcelain objects covered with little flowers and what is referred to as "moss" or "spinach." Produced in Germany, they come in shapes such as watering cans, baskets, swans, and shoes. The items below may or may not have been made specifically as toothpick holders, but the sizes are perfect and they find their way into our collections.

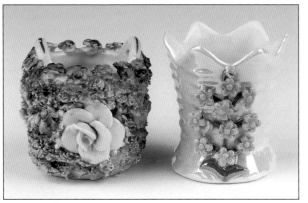

Fig. 292. *Left)* Basket. Marked – Elfinware, Germany. $25-35. *Right)* Basket weave; lustre; cluster of blue forget-me-nots. Marked – Germany. $20-30.

Fig. 293. *Left)* Delicate ruffled rim Marked – Germany. $25-35. *Right)* Four feet. Marked – Germany. $25-35.

Japan (Nippon)

Japan was one of the largest producers of toothpick holders, although the variety is not as great as what was produced in Germany. The Japanese or Nippon (the Japanese name for Japan) toothpick holders are fairly easy to find, but we do not know the manufacturer of many of them. There are a variety of marks found on these items, but they typically provide only the name of the country and, in some cases, the name of the importer for whom they were made. Several of the marks include the letter "M" in a wreath, which stands for Morimura Bros., the largest importer of Japanese wares for many years. Some of the older Japanese pieces are marked with Japanese characters that may represent the artist's name rather than the manufacturer, complicating identity even further. Manufacturer's marks associated with the toothpicks shown in this section are included at the end of the section.

The decoration on Japanese toothpick holders often has an "oriental" look, but not always. Because much of the ware was produced for exporting, the designs may give no clue as to their source of origin. The decoration can be minimal, or extremely detailed and artistic.

Nearly all of the early Japanese toothpick holders are hand painted, even the fairly common Geisha Girl types that were made to sell very inexpensively. Compare any two of them and you will see obvious differences even though the scene itself is the same. It was not uncommon for several members of a family to participate in decorating china. It was a family business. The quality of the decoration will vary from fairly crude, simple designs or scenes to highly detailed images, depending on the skill of the artist and the value placed on the end product.

Just as the decoration can vary from one extreme to the other, so does the quality of the ware produced. The less expensive china is quite porous and many impurities can be seen. It will also be fairly thick and "chunky" looking. The finer wares will be egg-shell thin with a very hard surface and a translucent quality. Typically, the decoration on these better pieces will also be of better quality. Royal Satsuma and Imperial Nippon are two names associated with better quality china.

Pieces made prior to 1891 or that were not intended for export may be marked with Japanese characters. With the passing of the McKinley Tariff act in 1891, all imported wares were required to be marked with the country of origin. It was at that point that the items were marked with the word Nippon, the Japanese name for their country. Later, in 1921, the U. S. Customs Bureau decided that Nippon was no longer acceptable and the name Japan had to be used. These changes provide some basis for determining the age of toothpicks produced in Japan.

A word of caution! Fake Japanese marks abound. To date, the only one we have seen on toothpicks is the Maple Leaf mark, but it is possible that the Rising Sun mark was also used since it has been found on a number of other items. Your best protection against this fraud is to know the shapes associated with contemporary toothpicks. Most are shown in the Contemporary Toothpick Holders chapter. An example of a fake Maple Leaf mark is shown below.

Fig. 294. Fake Nippon Maple Leaf mark.

Fig. 295. Similar in shape, highly decorated with a scene plus elaborate gold detail on sides and back. Very thin, translucent china, an example of the variations found in hand-painted decorations. Basic design is the same, background and remainder of the toothpick vary. Marked – Japanese characters, indicating early production. $55-75 each.

Fig. 296. *Left)* Geisha Girl. Traditional shape and color, poor quality. Marked – Made in Japan. $20-35. *Center)* Traditional colors, floral design less common. Unmarked. $30-40. *Right)* Geisha Girl. Traditional colors, less common shape. Unmarked. $30-40.

Fig. 297. *Left)* Geisha Girl. Blue is less common than the orange, corset shape. Unmarked. $30-40. *Center)* Floral. Heavier weight. Marked – Made in Japan. $30-40. *Right)* Geisha Girl. Less common blue, traditional shape. Marked – Japan. $35-45.

Fig. 298. *Left)* Barrel shape. Unmarked $35-50.
Right) Four lobes, larger size. Unmarked. $25-35.

Fig. 299. Three similar, but different three-lobe molds. *Left)* Cobalt trim, thinner, better quality china. Marked – Japanese characters. $30-40. *Center)* Mold detail not as well defined, but decoration is much more detailed, lesser quality china. Unmarked. $40-55. *Right)* Thin, fine quality china, minimal decoration. Marked – Japanese characters. $30-40.

Fig. 300. *Left)* Great decoration, home on water with enamel dots applied to trees. Marked – Made in Japan. $25-35. *Center)* Traditional shape, band of decoration at top. Marked – Made in Japan. $20-30. *Right)* Traditional shape with uncharacteristic decoration, blue bird in tree. Marked – Hand Painted, Japan in red banner. $25-35.

Fig. 301. *Left)* Hand painted. Unmarked. $25-30. *Center)* Rose bowl shape with four small feet. Unmarked. $25-40. *Right)* Shape similar to first one. Unmarked. $25-35.

Fig. 302. *Left)* Raised enamel decoration, detailed embossing on lower one third. Marked – Made in Japan. $35-45. *Right)* Similar shape, less detail on mold. Marked – Japan. $20-35.

Fig. 303. *Left)* Larger size, unusual shape. Unmarked. $35-50. *Right)* Wide-ribbed body, four small feet. Unmarked. $30-40.

Fig. 304. *Left)* Raised enamel decoration, three lobes, unusual shape. Marked – see Fig. 343. $45-60. *Right)* Translucent with a blue tinge. Marked – see Fig. 350. $30-40.

Fig. 305. *Left)* Three handles, gold trim. Marked – Japanese characters. $35-45. *Center)* Lustre interior. Marked – see Fig. 351. $25-35. *Right)* Hexagon shaped. Unmarked. $30-40.

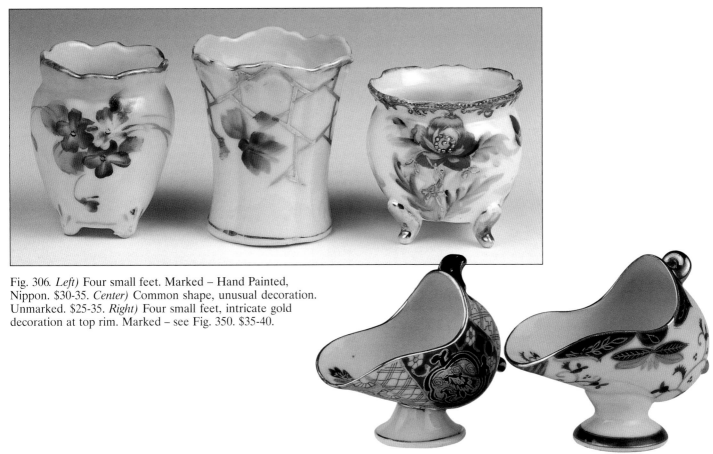

Fig. 306. *Left)* Four small feet. Marked – Hand Painted, Nippon. $30-35. *Center)* Common shape, unusual decoration. Unmarked. $25-35. *Right)* Four small feet, intricate gold decoration at top rim. Marked – see Fig. 350. $35-40.

Fig. 307. *Left)* Decorated inside. Marked – see Fig. 356. $25-40. *Right)* Slightly different shape, decorated inside. Marked – Hand Painted, Made in Japan. $25-35.

Fig. 308. Three similar, but different shapes. *Left)* Marked – Made in Japan. $25-40. *Center)* Marked – see Fig. 341. $25-35. *Right)* Heavily accented with gold. Marked – see Fig. 355. $35-50.

Fig. 309. Condiment set on tray. Excellent decoration with raised enamel accents. Marked – Made in Japan. $75-100 for the set.

Fig. 310. *Left)* Hand painted, similar to the next photo, but different. Unmarked. $40-55. *Center)* Hand painted, heavy gold decoration. Unmarked. $45-60. *Right)* Hand painted. Unmarked. $35-50.

Fig. 311. *Left)* Souvenir of the 1893 Chicago World's Fair, which is actually spelled out in the gold medallions. Rare, highly sought after World's Fair collectible. Unmarked. $275-350. *Right)* Unusual shape. Unmarked. $40-55.

Fig. 312. *Left)* Four feet, 1 7/8"
tall. Unmarked. $30-35. *Right)*
Marked – see Fig. 353. $30-40.

Fig. 313. *Left)* Eight sided.
Marked – see Fig. 349. $30-
40. *Center)* Gold band.
Marked – see Fig. 349. $25-
35. *Right)* Square. Marked –
see Fig. 349. $35-45.

Fig. 314. *Left)* Hexagonal.
Marked – see Fig. 350, green.
$30-40. *Center)* Round.
Marked – see Fig. 350, green.
$25-35. *Right)* Tree in
Meadow, popular pattern.
Marked – see Fig. 350, red.
$55-70.

Fig. 315. *Left)* Meito China.
Marked – see Fig. 357, also
known with Fig. 348. $30-45.
Right) Noritake. Marked –
see Fig. 350, green. $30-45.

Fig. 316. *Left)* Three handles. Marked – Nippon, wreath. $40-45.
Right) Tree scene. Marked – Nippon, green rising sun. $45-60.

Fig. 317. *Left)* Three handles, unusual shape. Marked – see Fig. 349. $20-30. *Center)*
Hand painted. Marked – blue "NORITAKE" in an arc above "NIPPON," registered in
Japan in 1911, one of the marks also used on undecorated wares exported to the United
States and other countries. $45-55. *Right)* Three handle. Marked – see Fig. 349. $35-45.

Fig. 318. Three small nub feet.
Marked – see Fig. 349. $25-35.

Fig. 319. Phoenix Bird, three ball feet.
Marked – see Fig. 349. $60-75.

Fig. 320. *Left)* Same shape as the glass pattern known as Atlas. Unmarked. $20-30. *Right)* Unusual shape and decoration for Nippon. Marked – see Fig. 344. $20-30.

Fig. 321. *Left)* Art Deco decoration, lustre ware. Marked – see Fig. 350. $50-65. *Right)* Flamingo dancer, popular decoration, lustre ware. Marked – see Fig. 350. $70-95.

Fig. 322. Condiment set, lustre ware. Salt, pepper, and toothpick are inserted into holder shaped like a boat. Marked – see Fig. 354. $75-95.

Fig. 323. Similar shapes, 3" tall. *Left)* Very detailed decoration, thin china. Marked – Japanese characters. $45-55. *Right)* Thin china, Moriage decoration. Unmarked. $45-65.

Fig. 324. Excellent quality Moriage.
Marked – see Fig. 342. $75-100.

Fig. 325. *Left)* Good quality with good decoration. Mark – Hand Painted Nippon
decal, Japanese characters. $45-55. *Center)* Good quality china and decoration.
Different floral on each side. Unmarked. $45-55. *Right)* Similar to the toothpick
on the left, but much heavier. Unmarked. $35-45:

Fig. 326. *Left)* Heavy raised gold detail. Unmarked. $40-45.
Right) Heavy gold detail. Unmarked. $40-45.

Fig. 327. Very ornate with attached
underplate. Unmarked. $45-55.

Fig. 328. *Left)* Band of flowers. Marked – Japan. $35-45. *Right)* Pretty hand painted flowers, uncommon shape. Unmarked. $35-45.

Fig. 329. *Left)* Matte finish with gold trim. Marked – see Fig. 349. $35-50. *Center)* Imperial Nippon. Three handles, three feet. Marked – see Fig. 337. $50-75. *Right)* Imperial Nippon. Three feet. Marked – see Fig. 337. $50-65.

Fig. 330. Royal Satsuma. *Left)* Hexagon shaped, very ornate, heavy gold. Marked – see Fig. 338. $55-65. *Right)* Round, ornate gold work. Marked – see Fig. 338. $55-65.

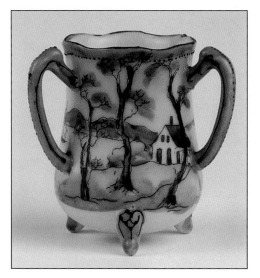

Fig. 331. Three handles, raised enamel. Marked – Made in Nippon. $45-60.

Fig. 332. Raised gold scrolling, two handles, four feet. Marked – Japan. $55-65.

Fig. 333. *Left)* Three handles, elaborate raised gold work. Marked – Hand Painted Nippon. $45-60. *Right)* Three handles, exquisite hand painting. Marked – see Fig. 342. $45-55.

Fig. 334. *Left)* Two handles, ornate raised gold. Marked – see Fig. 352. $45-60. *Right)* Three handles and feet, ornate gold. Marked – see Fig. 345. $45-60.

Fig. 335. *Left)* Two handles, four feet. Marked – see Fig. 349, blue. $35-45. *Right)* Heavily decorated with gold. Marked – see Fig. 340. $45-55.

Fig. 336. *Left)* Two handles, raised gold work. Marked – see Fig. 348. $45-55. *Right)* Three handles. Marked – see Fig. 343. $45-55.

Japanese Marks

Fig. 337. Imperial Nippon mark, better quality china. Dates unknown.

Fig. 338. Royal Satsuma mark, found on better quality china. Dates unknown.

Fig. 339. Tree mark, aka komaru c. 1906-1908. Symbolizes strength – to be strong, a tree must be equally balanced above and below ground.

Fig. 340. Pagoda mark. No information found.

Fig. 341. Rising Sun mark, blue c. 1890-1921. This mark has been reproduced. Sun's rays are represented by individual lines on the old mark.

Fig. 342. Maple Leaf mark, from 1891, associated with Moriumura Bros., Tokyo, in blue (first grade), green (second grade), and magenta. This mark has been reproduced. The leaf on the old mark is only about 1/4" in diameter, while it is about 1/2" in diameter on the new mark. Also see fig. 294.

Fig. 343. Cherry Blossom mark, known in blue, green, and magenta. Before 1921.

Fig. 344. Crown, Made in Nippon, before 1921.

Fig. 345. RC (Royal Ceramic) Nippon, issued in 1906, registered in Japan in 1911, both red and green used for wares exported to the United States.

Fig. 346. Green crown mark, before 1921.

Fig. 347. Nippon. Uncertain if name is CHICUSA or CHIC USA, c. 1880-1921.

Fig. 348. TN-in-wreath, green, before 1921.

Fig. 349. Nippon M-in-wreath, hand painted, most common mark, before 1921.

Fig. 350. Noritake M-in-wreath mark, M stands for Morimura Bros. importing company, green used from 1918-1941, red used from 1925-1941.

Fig. 351. M in open red wreath. No information found.

Fig. 352. Japan, Hand Painted. No information found.

Fig. 353. Double T Diamond mark, after 1921.

Fig. 354. Red circle with diamond shaped design in center, after 1921. No information found.

Fig. 355. Shofu mark, after 1921.

Fig. 356. Hokutosha, Made in Occupied Japan, c. 1945-1952.

Fig. 357. Meito China crown mark, after 1921.

Prussia

In a region of the German Empire known as Prussia, there were many porcelain companies that manufactured some of the finest porcelain ever made. Two separate families with the same last name of Schegelmilch produced the most famous and highest quality porcelain. The Erdmann Schlegelmilch (ES) family operated factories from 1861-1945. This includes operations by Carl Schlegelmilch (CS) and Oscar Schlegelmilch (OS), Erdmann's grandsons. Reinhold Schlegelmilch (RSP, RSG) factories were in operation from 1894-1945.

The term Prussia or RS Prussia has become synonymous with Reinhold Schlegelmilch's family, which exported their outstanding porcelain to the world. In this section we try to show many examples of Reinhold's toothpicks with the famous R. S. Prussia mark. Not to be ignored are the many pieces that were produced by the other Schlegelmilch factories.

There are numerous Prussia-related marks or backstamps in addition to the well-known R. S. Prussia wreath and star. It is interesting to note the trade names that were used – Royal Tillowitz, Royal Silesia, Royal Vienna, etc. – tended to make one think that "Royalty" was linked to the porcelain. According to *Caper's Notes on the Marks of Prussia*, the use of the term "Royal" was strictly a sales or promotional gimmick, which could have actually insulted the monarchy, but promoted "snob" appeal to a certain degree for Americans. Some ambiguous markings are the embossed stars, letters, bars, etc. Though unique to the porcelain, it is not known whether they were used to reinforce the bottom of the mold or for decoration. Though we identify them as such, they are not considered a true mark. You will find the marks grouped by manufacturer at the end of this section.

Beginning in the late 1880s up until the 1940s, you notice the style of the toothpick holders evolved with the demands of the times. Starting with simpler embossed molds, they evolved into elaborate designs with pedestals, fancy handles, and detailed transfers. This period is the most sought after. Then, the Art Deco period brought about the more sleek lines.

One wonderful aspect of Schlegelmilch porcelain is the transfer designs that were used. Though there were thousands, certain ones are particularly sought after by collectors. Portraits and scenes are the most popular and these, instead of the mold, can affect the price. As discussed in the German category, there were many blanks offered to the American porcelain painting craft. In this section you will also find several examples of hand painted porcelain.

Fortunately, there are very few reproduction china toothpick holders, but the R. S. Prussia mark has been faked. This new toothpick has the fake R. S. Prussia mark.

Fig. 358. This is a contemporary toothpick with a fake R.S. Prussia mark. Note the shape and the decoration so you will not be fooled. See Fig. 359.

Fig. 359. Fake R.S. Prussia mark. There are several fake marks being used on contemporary china. Compare this one closely with an authentic mark and you will notice that the top of the P does not extend to the left as it does on the original and there is no period after Prussia.

In our quest to photograph as many toothpick holders as possible, it was not always easy to photograph those from a single source together. Because of this, a few Prussia-related toothpicks are found in the German category. Please see Figures 224, 227, 248, 262, 268, 269, and 285.

We have provided drawings of many Prussian toothpicks in the Appendix. The mold details provided in these drawings may be helpful in identifying unmarked Prussian toothpicks.

Note: Toothpicks marked R. S. Germany or known to be R. S. Germany are included in this section as they were produced by the Prussia factories.

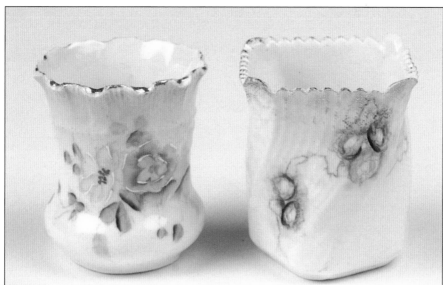

Fig. 360. *Left)* "Beaded Ruffle" mold 7. Unmarked. $40-60. *Right)* Mold 26. Unmarked. $40-60.

Fig. 361. Early mold. Unmarked. $40-60.

Fig. 362. *Left)* "Tree Bark" mold. Unmarked. $40-60 *Right)* ES mold. Unmarked. $40-60.

Fig. 363. *Left)* Swirl to base. Unmarked. $30-50. *Right)* Swirled to top, four feet. Mold A5. Unmarked. $30-50.

Fig. 364. *Left)* Three feet. Unmarked $45-65.
Right) Three feet. Unmarked. $30-60.

Fig. 365. *Left)* Mold 62. Unmarked. $40-60.
Right) Mold 30. Unmarked. $35-55.

Fig. 366. *Left)* Unusual leaf shaped base. Unmarked. $75-125.
Right) Ornate, gathered top. Mold 13. Unmarked. $45-65.

Fig. 367. *Left)* Unmarked. $40-60. *Right)*
Mold 50. Unmarked. $40-60.

Fig. 368. *Left)* OS related. Unmarked. $40-60.
Right) Ribbed, sterling rim. Unmarked. $40-60.

Fig. 369. *Left)* Mold 102. Marked – see Fig. 441. $50-60. *Right)* Heart shaped opening. Marked – see Fig. 441. $75-125.

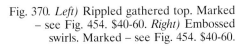

Fig. 370. *Left)* Rippled gathered top. Marked – see Fig. 454. $40-60. *Right)* Embossed swirls. Marked – see Fig. 454. $40-60.

Fig. 371. *Left)* "Tassel" mold. Unmarked. $30-50. *Center)* Known Prussia mold. Marked – blue castle, Made in Germany. $30-50. *Right)* Pink inside rim. Unmarked. $30-50.

Fig. 372. *Left)* "Cactus" mold. Unmarked. $35-55. *Right)* "Tree Trunk" mold. Unmarked. $35-55.

Fig. 373. *Left)* Possibly Prussia mold. Unmarked. $35-50. *Center)* Unmarked. $35-50. *Right)* "Candy Cane," mold 10. Unmarked. $45-65.

Fig. 374. *Left)* Mold 120. Unmarked. $40-60. *Center)* Square, four feet, mold 29. Unmarked. $40-60. *Right)* Unusual four lobed sections, embossed flower. Mold 152. Unmarked. $40-60.

Fig. 375. Early mold, orange inside top rim. Marked – see Fig. 440. $40-60.

Fig. 376. *Left)* Hand painted, artist signed "K. Rupp '46." Marked – see Fig. 452. $40-55. *Center)* Slight twist to mold, gold trim top. Marked – see Fig. 452. $40-55. *Right)* Marked – see Fig. 452. $40-55.

Fig. 377. *Left)* Hand painted. Marked – see Fig. 453. $40-55. *Center)* OS related mold. Unmarked. $40-55. *Right)* Marked – see Fig. 449. $35-45.

Fig. 378. Mold 373. Marked – see Fig. 443. $50-70.

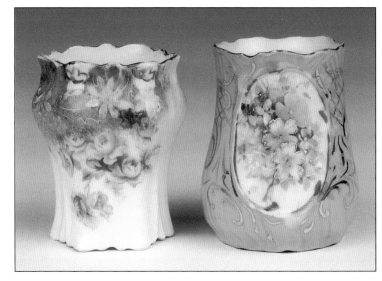

Fig. 379. *Left)* "Rosebud" mold 10. Marked – green Steeple mark. $100-150. *Right)* Mold 75. Sometimes found with ES mark, Fig. 450. $50-60.

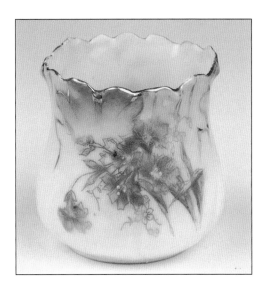

Fig. 380. Beautifully decorated early mold. Unmarked. Sometimes found with Steeple mark. $75-100.

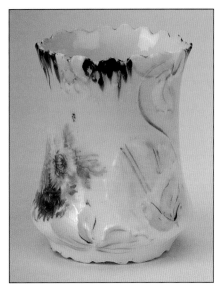

Fig. 381. Hidden Image mold with embossed lady's profile in the lower right. Rare. Unmarked. $400-500.

Fig. 382. *Left)* Mold 7. Marked – see Fig. 442. $100-150. *Right)* Unusual pierced base, mold 14. Marked – see Fig. 442. $100-150.

Fig. 383. *Left)* Skirted floral, mold 524. Unmarked. $50-60. *Right)* Pink floral. Marked – see Fig. 439. $50-60.

Fig. 384. *Left)* "Grape Leaf" mold. Unmarked. $45-65. *Center)* Unmarked. $50-75. *Right)* Unmarked. $35-50.

Fig. 386. *Left)* ES transfer, "Summer Portrait." Unmarked. $45-60. *Right)* Marked – see Fig. 451. $50-100.

Fig. 385. ES transfer, "Winter Portrait." Unmarked. $40-60.

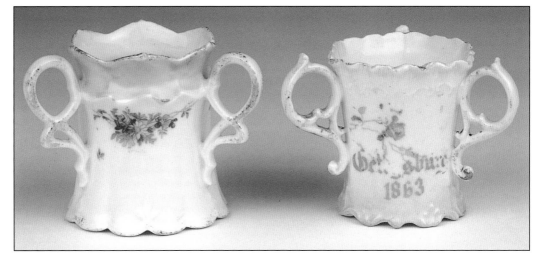

Fig. 387. *Left)* Three handles, possibly early Prussia. Unmarked. $150-225. *Right)* Three handles, souvenir of "Gettysburg 1863," very unusual to find this item as a souvenir. Floral design on other sides. Marked – see Fig. 439. $150-225.

Fig. 388. Early star marked molds. *Left)* Three handles, mold 140. Marked – see Fig. 439. $100-125. *Right)* Raised enamel detail. Mold 150a. Marked – see Fig. 439. $75-125.

Fig. 389. *Left)* Three handles, mold 545. Unmarked. $150-225. *Right)* Sometimes found with ES Prov Saxe mark, see Fig. 452. Unmarked. $75-125.

Fig. 390. *Left)* Mold 130. Unmarked. $75-125. *Center)* Pedestal, mold 12. Scarce. Unmarked. $200-275. *Right)* Mold 504. Bows loop around as handles. Unmarked. $150-250.

Fig. 391. *Left)* Mold 61. Unmarked. $55-75. *Right)* Marked – see Fig. 446. $40-60.

Fig. 392. *Left)* Large chrysanthemum. Marked – see Fig. 452. $65-85. *Right)* Floral. Marked – see Fig. 452. $65-85.

Fig. 393. *Left)* Wonderful hand painting, mold 521. Unmarked. $175-225. *Right)* Three handles, hand painted, mold 502. Unmarked. $200-250.

Fig. 394. *Left)* Three handles, mold 502. Unmarked. $200-250. *Right)* Three handle, mold 509. Marked – see Fig. 444. $200-250.

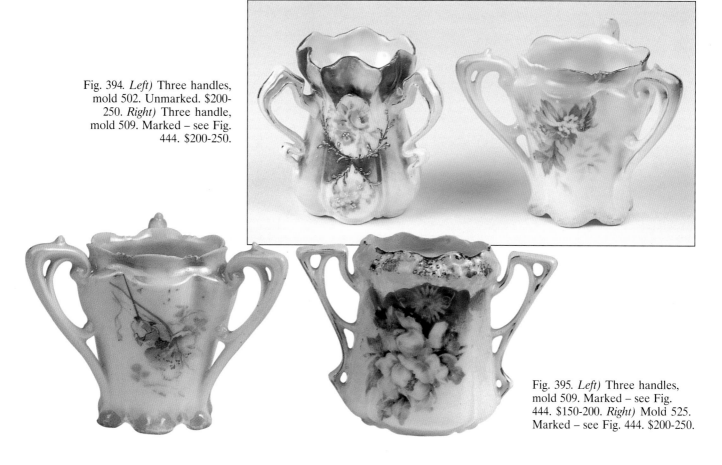

Fig. 395. *Left)* Three handles, mold 509. Marked – see Fig. 444. $150-200. *Right)* Mold 525. Marked – see Fig. 444. $200-250.

Fig. 396. *Left)* Three handles, mold 511. Unmarked. $200-250. *Right)* Three handles, mold 501. Unmarked. $200-250.

111

Fig. 397. *Left)* Three handle, mold 511. Unmarked. $200-250. *Right)* Three handle, mold 529. Unmarked. $200-250.

Fig. 398. *Left)* Three handles, mold 627. Detailed gold scrolling. Unmarked. $200-250. *Right)* Three handles, hand painted mold 529. Unmarked. $150-200.

Fig. 400. *Left)* "Icicle" mold 641, two handles. Unmarked. $200-250. *Right)* Three handles, embossed flower. Unmarked. $125-150.

Fig. 399. Mold 475, this example is rare with factory decoration and RSP mark - see Fig. 444. Usually found blank or hand painted with blue RSG mark. $250-350.

Fig. 401. *Left)* Three handles, very detailed thin porcelain. Possibly Prussia related. Unmarked. $100-125. *Right)* Three handles, possibly Prussia related. Unmarked. $125-150.

Fig. 403. *Left)* Mold 636. Unmarked. $150-225.
Right) White iris, mold 454. Unmarked. $150-200.

Fig. 402. Mold 542, three handles. Exceptional hand painting, artist signed "F. Austin." Unmarked. $300-350.

Fig. 404. *Left)* Mold 584. Marked – see Fig. 444. $175-225.
Right) "Jewel" mold 643. Marked – see Fig. 444. $200-250.

Fig. 405. "Jewel" mold 645, notice the "jewels" at top decorated as opals. Original paper label "Made in Germany." Marked – see Fig. 444. $250-300.

Fig. 406. *Left)* Satin finish, mold 458. Marked – see Fig. 444. $125-175. *Right)* Mold 537. Marked – see Fig. 444. $200-225.

Fig. 407. *Left)* Mold 12. Marked – see Fig. 442. $400-450. *Right)* Mold 536. Marked – see Fig. 444. $250-300.

Fig. 408. *Left)* Detailed gold decoration. Mold 648. Marked – see Fig. 444. $200-250. *Right)* Mold 636. Marked – see Fig. 444. $200-250.

Fig. 409. *Left)* Mold 543. Unmarked. $125-175. *Right)* Mold 540a. Unmarked. $150-225.

Fig. 410. *Left)* Mold 609. Marked – see Fig. 444. $275-325. *Right)* Mold 566. Marked – see Fig. 444. $275-325.

Fig. 411. *Left)* Mold 608. Rare. Marked – see Fig. 444. $350-450. *Right)* Beautiful detailed decoration, mold 664. Rare. Unmarked. $400-425.

Fig. 412. *Left)* Three handles, dramatic gold work. Marked – RSG, red wreath. $100-150. *Right)* Three handles, luster finish. Mold 580. Marked – RSG, red wreath. $150-175.

Fig. 413. *Left)* "Cottage" scene, mold 580. Unmarked. $275-300. *Right)* "Black Duck and Pine Trees" scene, mold 631. Rare. Marked – see Fig. 444. $400-600.

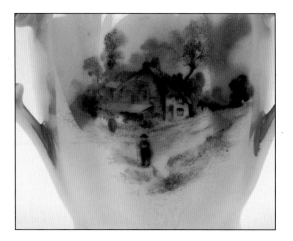

Fig. 414. Three handles, "Castle" scene, mold 580. Unmarked. $275-325.

Fig. 415. *Left)* Three handles, mold 580. "Farm" scene transfer, see Fig. 416. Unmarked. $275-300. *Right)* Three handles, mold 580. "Country House by Lake" transfer, see Fig. 417. Unmarked. $275-300.

Fig. 416. Mold 580 with scarce "Farm" scene transfer.

Fig. 417. Mold 580 with scarce "Country House by Lake" transfer.

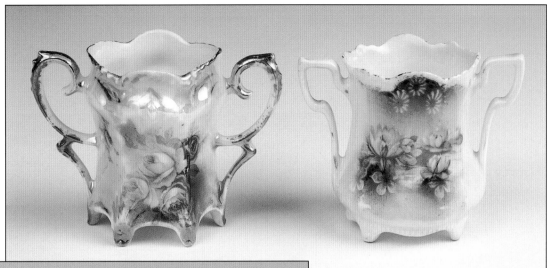

Fig. 418. *Left)* "Jewel" mold 642. Unmarked. $200-250. *Right)* "Reflecting Water Lilies" scene, "Medallion" mold 631. Unmarked. $200-250.

Fig. 419. *Left)* Mold 517. Unmarked. $225-275. *Right)* "Carnation" mold 526. Marked – see Fig. 444. $225-275.

Fig. 420. *Left)* Mold 517. Unmarked. $225-275. *Right)* "Plume" mold 658. Marked – see Fig. 444. $200-225.

Fig. 421. *Left)* Mold 644. Marked – see Fig. 444. $200-250. *Right)* Mold 480. Marked – see Fig. 444. $250-300.

Fig. 422. *Left)* "Iris" mold 628. Marked – see Fig. 444. $225-275. *Right)* Mold 644. Marked – see Fig. 444. $175-225.

Fig. 423. *Left)* Three handles, elaborate gold. Mold 61. Unmarked. $175-225. *Right)* Ruffled top, mold 502. Unmarked. $100-150.

Fig. 424. *Left)* Three handles, mold 510. Marked – see Fig. 444. $150-200. *Right)* Three handles, mold 61. Marked – see Fig. 444. $150-200.

Fig. 425. *Left)* Three handles, very detailed mold 6. Unmarked. $125-150. *Right)* Hand painted, mold 510. Unmarked. $100-150.

Fig. 426. *Left)* Unusual three handles. Marked – see Fig. 446. $75-100. *Right)* Hexagon shaped. Marked – see Fig. 446. $75-100.

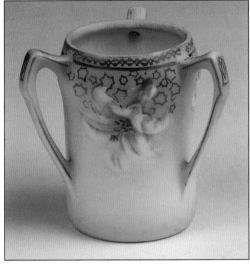

Fig. 427. Three handle Art Nouveau design. Marked – see Fig. 446. $125-150.

Fig. 428. *Left)* Marked- see Fig. 446. $75-85. *Right)* Three gathered handles with underplate. Marked – see Fig. 446. $75-85.

Fig. 429. *Left)* Hand painted floral, mold 656. Marked – see Fig. 446. $60-80. *Right)* Poppy. Marked – see Fig. 446. $60-80.

Fig. 430. *Left)* Hand painted floral, mold 476. Marked – see Fig. 446. $75-100. *Right)* Pink roses. Marked – see Fig. 446. $75-100.

Fig. 431. *Left)* Three handles. Marked – see Fig. 446. $100-125. *Right)* Three handles, mold 579. Marked – see Fig. 446. $100-125.

Fig. 432. *Left)* Large rose. Marked – see Fig. 445. $100-125. *Right)* Three handles. Marked – Germany. $100-125.

Fig. 433. *Left)* Hexagon shaped with leaves. Marked – see Fig. 447. $65-75. *Right)* Hexagon shaped, blue rim. Marked – blue wreath, R.S. Tillowitz. $65-75.

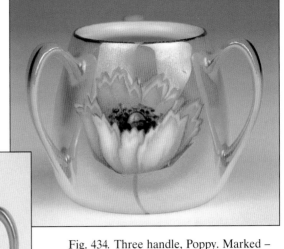

Fig. 434. Three handle, Poppy. Marked – see Fig. 448. This mold often seen with RSG blue wreath mark. $175-200.

Fig. 435. *Left)* Three handles, hand painted, mold 475. Marked – RSG, blue wreath. $75-125. *Right)* Hand painted, mold 486. Marked – RSG, blue wreath. $75-125.

Fig. 436. *Left)* Hand painted Art Deco. Marked – RSG, blue wreath. $75-100. *Right)* Six sided angles. Marked – RSG, blue wreath. $75-100.

Fig. 437. Three handles, monogram. Marked – "Hand Painted Rogers-Martini Co" in circle and RSG blue wreath mark. $50-75.

Fig. 438. Royal Rudolstadt. Art Nouveau design. Marked – see Fig. 455. $125-175.

121

Fig. 439. Embossed star. Reinhold Schlegelmilch Porcelain Factories, c. 1890 – 1917.

Fig. 440. Shell mark. Reinhold Schlegelmilch Porcelain Factories, c. 1888 – 1894.

Fig. 441. Wing mark. Reinhold Schlegelmilch Porcelain Factory, c. 1880-1900.

Fig. 442. Steeple mark. Reinhold Schlegelmilch Porcelain Factories, c. 1894-1917.

Fig. 443. SAXE ALTENBURG, trade name used by Reinhold Schlegelmilch Porcelain Factories, c. 1900.

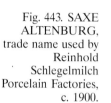

Fig. 444. RS Prussia (RSP) red and green wreath and star mark. Reinhold Schlegelmilch Porcelain Factories, c. 1898-1917. This mark can be found with slight variations.

Fig. 445. Reinhold Schlegelmilch Porcelain Factory, Tillowitz, c. 1905-1945.

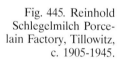

Fig. 446. RS Germany (RSG) green wreath and star mark. Reinhold Schlegelmilch Porcelain Factories, c. 1913-1945.

Fig. 447. Reinhold Schlegelmilch Porcelain Factory, Tillowitz, c. 1920 – 1945.

Fig. 448. Royal Silesia, trade name used by Reinhold Schlegelmilch Porcelain Factories, c. 1900.

Fig. 449. Erdmann Schlegelmilch Porcelain Factory, c. pre-1900.

Fig. 450. Erdmann Schlegelmilch Porcelain Factory, Suhl, c. 1888-1900.

Fig. 451. Erdmann Schlegelmilch Porcelain Factory, c. 1900.

Fig. 452. Erdmann Schlegelmilch Porcelain Factory, Suhl, c. 1900 -1930.

Fig. 453. Carl Schlegelmilch Porcelain Factory, c. 1883-1918.

Fig. 454. Oscar Schlegelmilch Porcelain Factory, Thuringia, Germany, c. 1892-1925.

Fig. 455. Royal Rudolstadt / Prussia above crown mark. Beyer & Bock – Prussia, c. 1905-1931. Not Schlegelmilch related.

United States

Few china toothpicks were made in the United States during the peak of their popularity. Most were imported from Europe and Japan, as was the trend of the day. Later, in the 1920s-1940s, some companies produced them as part of their dinnerware lines, but even then there were not many made, as toothpick holders were no longer in vogue.

What did happen during the late 1880s and up until the 1920s was the importing of china blanks from various European manufacturers. These were made available both to professional decorating enterprises and to individuals who enjoyed the china painting hobby. For this reason, you will often see toothpick shapes associated with a particular company or region in Europe, but they will bare the mark of an American company or the name of an American artist.

One of the most popular decorating firms was Pickard. Wilder A. Pickard came from a family with artistic talent. He worked at a number of different positions during the difficult depression years, and then in 1897 began to focus exclusively on decorating china. His previous positions had provided a good background for venturing into his own china decorating business in Chicago, where he was able to recruit talented artists from among the immigrant population. Pickard decorated blanks made by some of the finest porcelain manufacturers in Europe. The business prospered and quickly became well known for excellent quality hand painted china. The company remains in business today.

Fig. 456. Manufactured by Ceramic Art Co., Trenton, NJ, c. 1894-1906 (now Lenox). Made to simulate the famous Irish Belleek soft-paste porcelain. Considered the highest achievement of American porcelain. Toothpicks are scarce. Marked – see Fig. 457. $100-150.

Fig. 457. Ceramic Art Co., Trenton, NY, c. 1894-1903.

Fig. 458. Silver overlay. Marked – see Fig. 459. $45-55.

Fig. 459. EAM Co., Electrolytic, Trenton, NJ. Possibly decorator. No information found.

Fig. 461. J. H. Stouffer Company (1905-1952), c. 1938-1946.

Fig. 460. *Left)* Pickard. Known as encrusted gold or all-over-gold (aog), Rose and Daisy. Unmarked. $75-125. *Right)* Stouffer Decorating company, Poppy. Marked – see Fig. 461. $75-125.

Fig. 463. Pickard, Chicago, Illinois, c. 1898.

Fig. 462. *Left)* Pickard, three feet. Marked- see Fig. 463. $100-140. *Right)* Pickard, two handles. Mold also found marked KPM Germany. Marked – see Fig. 463. $100-130.

Fig. 465. Pickard. Date uncertain, probably 1930s.

Fig. 464. Pickard. *Left)* Marked – see Fig. 465. $75-125. *Right)* Aster field. Marked – see Fig. 465. $75-125.

Fig. 466. Royal Crest
Porcelain. Marked –
see Fig. 467. $20-30.

Fig. 467. Royal Crest
Porcelain, Oakland,
Oregon. No information
found.

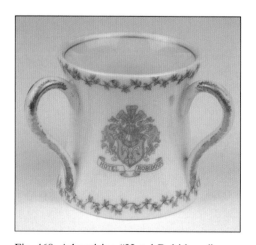

Fig. 468. Advertising "Hotel Robidoux."
Marked – O.P. Co. Syracuse China. $45-65.

Souvenir Toothpick Holders

Souvenir China was so popular with Americans between 1890 and 1930, that you can find pieces with landmarks or events from almost any town or city. All types of small items were made besides toothpick holders. Most are cobalt blue, but sepia drawings on white and other colors are found.

Most souvenir toothpicks are marked and, in some cases, they have marks representing both the manufacturer and the importer. The main importers were C. E. Wheelock & Co. and B. F. Hunt & Sons, though there were many others.

A unique feature is a backstamp featuring the town or merchant for which the item was made. Even though many of these businesses and landmarks no longer exist, having these items gives one a glimpse of the past.

Fig. 469. *Left)* Cobalt souvenir "Battery Park Hotel, Asheville, NC." Marked – Germany. $35-45. *Center)* Cobalt souvenir "Court House, Carrollton, GA." Marked – Germany. $35-45. *Right)* Cobalt souvenir "Public School, Morganton, WV." Marked – Wheelock Germany. $35-45.

Fig. 470. *Left)* Souvenir of "Toas Indian Pueblo, Taos, New Mexico." Marked – Made in Germany for the Remsberg Merc. Co., Raton, N.M. $30-45. *Center)* Souvenir of "Public School Building, Jewell City, Kans." Marked – Made in Germany for the I. D. Robertson Mer. Co., Jewell City, Kans." $30-45. *Right)* Souvenir of "Webster's Birthplace, Franklin, N.H." Marked – Made in Germany for F. M. Gerry, Franklin, NH. $30-45.

Fig. 471. Old Man of the Mountain, a famous mountain rock formation that became an enduring symbol of the State of New Hampshire, collapsed due to bad weather in 2003 and probably cannot be repaired. Very delicate china. Marked – gold script "China Hand Painted Made in Germany." $45-55.

Fig. 472. *Left)* Souvenir "Some of the Fishing SCHRS / Freeport NJ" Marked – Made in Germany, circle. $45-55. *Center)* Souvenir "Revere Beach." Marked – Made in Germany, circle. $30-40. *Right)* Souvenir "Old Orchard Beach." Marked – Dresden Wheelock. $30-45.

Fig. 473. *Left)* Souvenir of "College Chapel Building, Indianola, Iowa" Marked – circle, Made in Germany. $25-35. *Center)* Souvenir of "City Park and Lake, Glenwood, Iowa." Marked – Made in Germany for the Fair Store, Glenwood, Iowa. $25-35. *Right)* Souvenir of "Boston, Mass." Marked – circle, Made in Germany. $25-35.

Fig. 475. *Left)* Souvenir of "Carnegie Library, Tecumseh, Built 1904." Unmarked. $25-45. *Right)* Souvenir of "Bear River, N.S." Marked – see Fig. 476. $25-45.

Fig. 474. Souvenir of "Anaconda, MT." Marked – Made in Germany for Copper City Commercial. $45-60.

Fig. 476. This mark found on Prussia related molds. Note the word "in" is in the center and there is a tiny star in the circle.

Fig. 477. *Left)* Souvenir of a rock formation, "Rocks, Hopewell Cape, N.H." Unmarked. $25-45. *Right)* Souvenir of "South Boulder Canon, Colorado Springs, Colorado." Unmarked. $25-45.

Fig. 479.
Mitterteich
Porcelain Factory,
c. 1918.

Fig. 478. *Left)* Souvenir "Atlantic City." Marked – Made in Germany. $25-40. *Right)* Souvenir "Niagara Falls." Marked – see Fig. 479. $25-40.

Fig. 480. *Left)* Souvenir "Vicksburg, Ms." Unmarked. $30-50. *Center)* Souvenir "Sarcoxie, MO." Marked – Wheelock Germany. $30-50. *Right)* Souvenir "Niagara Falls." Marked – Made in Germany. $30-50.

Fig. 481. *Left)* Cobalt souvenir "Court House, Waterloo, Iowa." Marked – Germany. $25-35. *Center)* Yellow souvenir "Gary, In." Marked – Germany. $25-35. *Right)* Cobalt souvenir "Gale Memorial, Laconia, NH." Unmarked. $25-35.

Fig. 482. *Left)* Souvenir of "Catalina Ca." Marked – see Fig. 483. $25-35. *Center)* Souvenir "Bakers Hotel / Mineral Well, TX." Marked – Made in Germany. $25-35. *Right)* Souvenir "Cascade Gardens / St Louis Exposition 1904." Marked – Victoria, Austria. $25-35.

Fig. 483. Royal Rothenburg, JHR & Co., Germany. No information found.

Fig. 484. "XXth Anniversary, Syracuse Camera Club, Jan. 5, 1906" on the back side. Unmarked. $75-100.

Fig. 485. Denmark souvenir. "Welcome to Copenhagen." $30-45.

Sanitary Toothpick Holders

This type of holder was devised so that you pick the toothpicks up in the middle, keeping the ends untouched. Because of this they were dubbed "sanitary" and became very popular in the hotel and restaurant trade, since there the toothpicks were exposed to the public. They often served a dual purpose in that they would be used for advertising. You will find them from an array of different countries, making them a unique collectible.

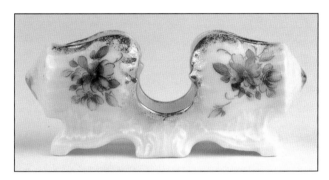

Fig. 486. Unique mold. Marked – see Fig. 8. $25-45.

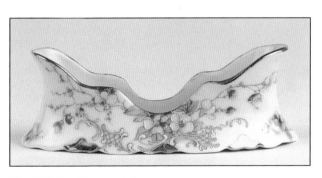

Fig. 487. Quality porcelain.
Marked – see Fig. 488. $45-55.

Fig. 488. Heinrich & Co.,
Bavaria, c. 1911.

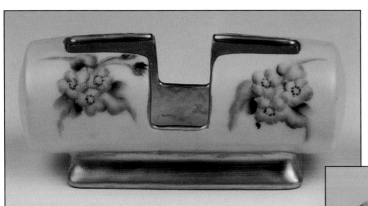

Fig. 489. Hand painted. Marked – Bavaria, shield. Thomas Marktredwitz Porcelain Factory, Bavaria, c. 1908. $35-45.

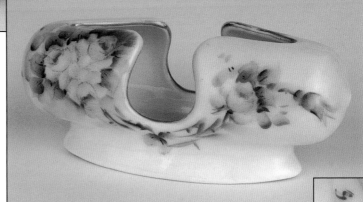

Fig. 490. Pink and white roses. Marked – see Fig. 491. $45-55.

Fig. 491. Jaeger & Company, Marktredwitz, Bavaria, c. 1902.

Fig. 492. Blue Onion type. Marked – Victoria under crown. Schmidt & Co. Porcelain Factory, Czechoslovakia, c. 1918-1939. $40-50.

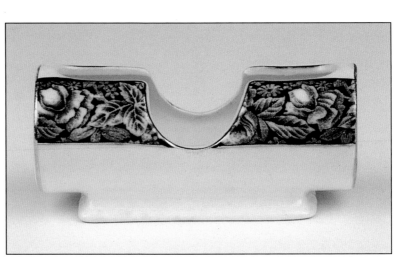

Fig. 493. Marked – ENGLAND with a ship in a square. $35-50.

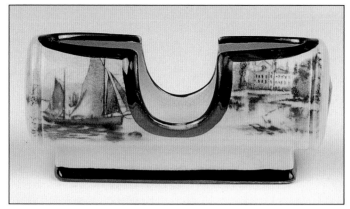

Fig. 494. Copper trim. Marked – England Ridgeway, crossed swords. $45-55.

Fig. 495. Blue transferware. Marked – Sydney British Anchor, England. $40-50.

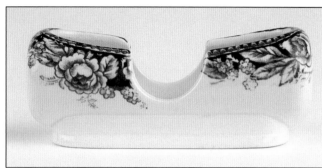

Fig. 496. *Left)* Hand painted. Marked – Limoges, star. $ 35-55. *Right)* Hand painted. Marked – Limoges, star. $35-55.

Fig. 497. *Left)* Marked – Weiden, Germany in oval. Bauscher Porcelain Factory, c. 1920. $25-35. *Right)* Marked – Weiden, Germany in oval. Bauscher Porcelain Factory, c. 1920. $30-40.

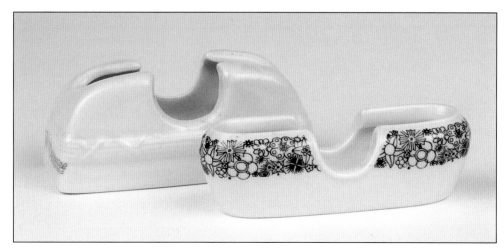

Fig. 498. *Left)* Advertising "Fraureuth." $30-40. *Right)* Marked – Bauser & Weiden. $30-40.

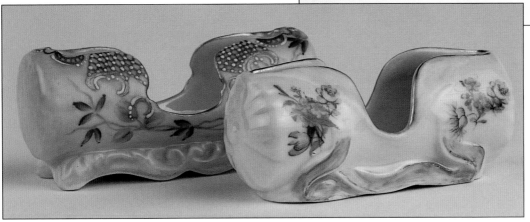

Fig. 499. *Left)* Unmarked. $45-55. *Right)* Marked – C.T. under eagle. C. Tielsch & Co. Silesia, Germany, c. 1934. $45-55.

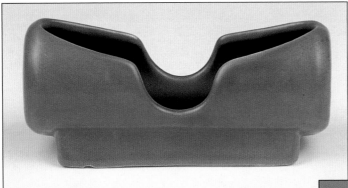

Fig. 500. Marked – Greece, bull in square. $35-45.

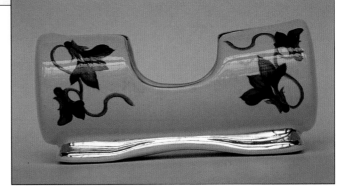

Fig. 501. Unmarked. $25-35.

134

Fig. 502. Hand painted, signed
"Golding." Unmarked. $35-45.

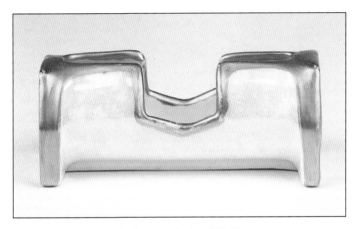

Fig. 503. Lustre. Marked – see Fig. 28. $35-45.

Fig. 504. *Left)* Hand painted.
Unmarked. $35-45. *Right)* Hand
painted. Unmarked. $35-45.

Fig. 505. *Left)* Marked – crown, Alfred
Meakin, England. $25-35. *Right)* Floral
also inside. Unmarked. $45-55.

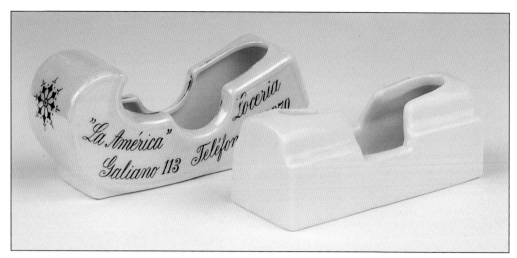

Fig. 506. *Left)* Gondola shaped, advertisement. Unmarked. $30-40. *Right)* Unusual shape. Unmarked. $30-40.

Fig. 507. *Left)* Advertising sanitary. Unmarked. $30-40. *Right)* Advertising sanitary. Unmarked. $30-40.

Fig. 508. Advertising "Chapultepec," possibly a restaurant. Unmarked. $35-50.

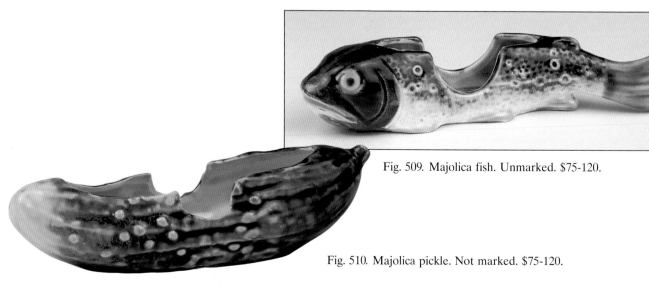

Fig. 509. Majolica fish. Unmarked. $75-120.

Fig. 510. Majolica pickle. Not marked. $75-120.

Figural Toothpick Holders

This category could be quite large, though we have limited it to the examples shown. Many figurals were made in Germany, but most are not marked, making research difficult. They can be found shaped like animals, humans, and inanimate object. They range from whimsical to the more serious. It is often overlooked that there was much artwork involved. All the painting and details, such as delicate facial features, were done by hand. Credit must also be given to the artists who created the image.

There is always the question with porcelain figurals as to whether they were really intended for toothpicks or just a what-not to sit on a shelf. A good rule of thumb is whether the holder or bowl can hold the toothpicks adequately. We also look inside to see if the "holder" is a cup-like shape with smooth sides or if it is irregular in form, taking the shape of the figurine. The latter was probably not intended as a toothpick.

Fig. 511. *Left)* Unmarked. $35-45. *Right)* Unmarked. $45-55.

Fig. 512. Bisque. Unmarked. $45-55.

Fig. 513. Nodder or bobble-head. Young girl drinking tea. Both head and legs move. Unmarked. $85-125.

Fig. 514. *Left)* Blond child, flowers applied to egg-shaped holder. Unmarked. $45-55. *Right)* Girl feeding blue bird, flower and leaves applied to holder. Marked – Shield mark. $45-55.

Fig. 515. Bisque. Unmarked. $40-55.

Fig. 516. Owl in Tree Stump by Hermann Ohme Porcelain Manufactory (1882-1930). Also made in a thicker, lower quality version by an unknown manufacturer. Unmarked. $65-75.

Fig. 517. Unmarked. Possibly Schafer & Vater. $45-55.

138

Fig. 518. *Left)* Unmarked. $35-50. *Right)* Marked – Duppel-Mohle. $25-35.

Fig. 519. *Left)* Good quality bisque. Unmarked. $45-55. *Center)* Marked – Japan. $20-30. *Right)* Marked – Japan. $25-35.

Fig. 520. Figural face. Unmarked. $25-35.

Fig. 521. Advertising for "CD Kenny Co," c. 1890-1934. CD Kenny used advertising give-a-ways for his grocery stores. Unmarked. $20-30.

Fig. 522. Top Hats. *Left)* Scene of building. Marked – Made in Germany. $35-50. *Right)* Floral. Unmarked. $35-50.

Fig. 523. Top Hats. *Left)* Dove on brim. Unmarked. $25-35. *Right)* Cameo. Marked – see Fig. 524. $30-40.

Fig. 524. Royal Blue Medallion, Germany. No information found.

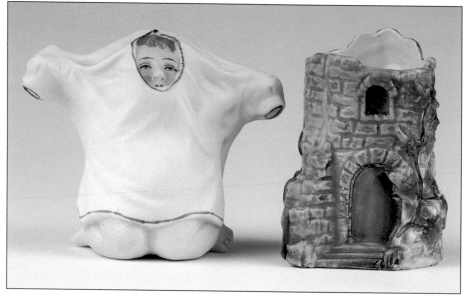

Fig. 525. Bohne. *Left)* Bisque. Marked – see Fig. 527. $55-65. *Right)* Bisque. Marked – see Fig. 527. $55-65.

Fig. 526. Bohne. See Fig. 527. $75-100.

Fig. 527. Ernest Bohne Sons, Germany, c. 1887-1920.

Fig. 528. Unmarked. $25-35.

Fig. 529. *Left)* Bisque. Marked – number. $30-40.
Right) Bisque. Marked – Japan. $25-35.

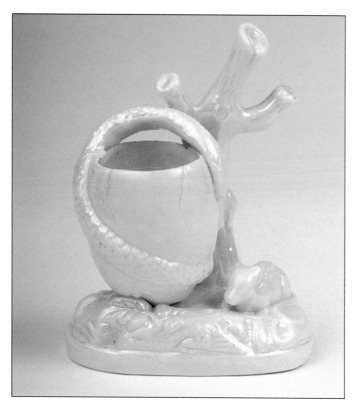

Fig. 531. Scottie dog, originally had red leather collar. Japanese. Unmarked. $30-40.

Fig. 530. Glossy finish, snake wrapped around egg and tree limb, rat on ground. Unmarked. $30-40.

Fig. 532. *Left)* Unmarked. $25-35. *Center)* Unmarked. $25-35. *Right)* Unmarked. $30-35.

Fig. 533. *Left)* Lustre. Marked – Made in Japan. $25-35. *Right)* Lustre. Unmarked. $25-35.

Fig. 534. *Left)* Unmarked. $30-40. *Right)* Unmarked. $35-45.

Fig. 535. Bisque. Unmarked. $65-75.

Fig. 536. *Left)* Unmarked. $20-30. *Right)* Marked – Wade, England. $20-30.

Fig. 537. Great detail. Marked – Japanese characters. $50-65.

Fig. 538. *Left)* Fish. Unmarked. $20-30.
Right) Cat. Marked – Tri China. $20-30.

Fig. 539. *Left)* Bisque.
Marked – Quality Guarantee.
$20-35. *Right)* Bisque.
Marked – number. $20-35.

Pink Pigs

Pink Pigs with cabbage green were made in Germany for the souvenir trade. Some made as toothpick holders, they are a highly sought after collectible. You will find them with as many as three pigs. The pigs may be in various poses or involved in an activity, the action ones being the most popular. Many of these were made. We show only a sampling of them here.

Fig. 540. *Left)* Unmarked. $30-45. *Right)* Unmarked. $45-65.

Fig. 541. *Left)* Marked – see Fig. 476.
$45-60. *Right)* Unmarked. $70-90.

Fig. 542. *Left)* Unmarked. $70-
90. *Right)* Unmarked. $45-55.

Fig. 543. *Left)* Unmarked. $45-55.
Right) Unmarked. $65-80.

Fig. 544. *Left)* Marked – see Fig. 476.
$45-55. *Right)* Unmarked. $75-100.

Miscellaneous Toothpick Holders

Included in this chapter are toothpicks from those countries where we had only a couple of examples, those with unusual treatments or finishes, and those that are unidentified.

Fig. 545. Marked – Made in China, acid etched. $15-25.

Fig. 546. Bing & Grondahl. *Left)* Seagulls. Marked – see Fig. 547. $70-85. *Right)* Marked – see Fig. 548. $65-75.

Fig. 547. Bing & Grondahl Porcelain Company, Copenhagen, Denmark, c. 1962.

Fig. 548. Bing & Grondahl Porcelain Company, Copenhagen, Denmark, c. 1970.

Fig. 549. Marked – Gouda. $75-85.

Fig. 551. Sabot mark.
No information found.

Fig. 550. Marked – see Fig. 551. $50-65.

Fig. 552. *Left)* Fine cream colored porcelain.
Marked -Zsolnay, Hungary. $35-45. *Right)*
Shamrocks. Marked – Herend, Hungary. $35-45.

Fig. 553. Belleek. Marked –
see Fig. 554. $75-95.

Fig. 554. Belleek
Pottery Co.,
Fermanagh, Ireland,
c. 1927.

Fig. 555. Wade Heath. *Left)*
Listed as a violet bowl.
Marked – Made in Ireland,
Shamrock, c. 1850-1986. $25-
30. *Right)* Marked – Made in
Ireland, Shamrock, c. 1850-
1986. $20-30.

Fig. 556. *Left)* Marked – Made in Italy. $45-55. *Right)* Capo-di-Monte. Marked – see Fig. 557. $55-65.

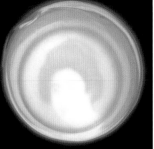

Fig. 557. Capo-di-monte, Made in Italy. The crown over the letter N was originally used by the Capo-di-Monte factory in Naples, Italy. This mark appears to be associated with the Societa Ceramica Richard (Richard-Ginori), Milan, Italy, in that it is very similar to several of their marks. No date known.

Fig. 559. Actual lithopane.

Fig. 558. Lithopane or Lithophane. Picture of Oriental lady in bottom of toothpick created using varying thicknesses of porcelain, visible only when light passes through it. See Fig. 559. $65-75

Fig. 560. *Left)* Majolica. Unmarked. $65-85. *Right)* Majolica. Unmarked. $70-95.

Fig. 561. Majolica. Un-marked. $65-85.

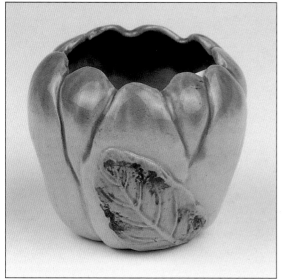

Fig. 562. Majolica leaf and stem. Unmarked. $40-50.

Fig. 563. *Left)* Sanded finish. Unmarked. $25-40. *Center)* Sanded finish. Unmarked. $25-40. *Right)* Copper lustre and sanded finish. Unmarked. $25-35.

Fig. 564. *Left)* Sanded finish. Unmarked. $25-35. *Right)* Sanded finish. Unmarked. $25-35.

Fig. 565. Copper lustre. Unmarked. $35-55.

Fig. 566. *Left)* Torquay Pottery, England. Motto ware, decorated with heavy slip, verses or sayings scratched through the slip to expose the redware beneath. "Be good and you will always be happy." Artists name not legible. Unmarked. $45-55. *Right)* Longwy Pottery. Millefiore pattern, also made with yellow background. Marked – Longwy Faience Co., France, Millefiore. $65-75.

Fig. 567. Keyhole cuts. Beautiful delicate china. *Left)* Unmarked. $75-100. *Right)* Unmarked. $75-100.

Fig. 568. Hand painted, beautiful gold work. Unmarked. $45-65.

Fig. 569. Two handles. Possibly Pickard or R.S. Germany. $75-95.

Fig. 570. Chintz with bird.
Unmarked. $50-65.

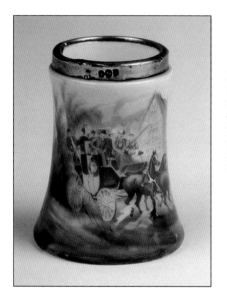

Fig. 571. Coach
transfer, very similar
to Royal Bayreuth
decorations, but not
positively attributed
to Royal Bayreuth.
Sterling rim.
Unmarked. $50-65.

Fig. 572. Blue Onion pattern attributed
to both Royal Bayreuth (Tettau), Royal
Copenhagen, and possibly other companies. This shape is like the German Delft
toothpicks, Fig. 230. $55-65.

Fig. 573. Blue Onion type. *Left)* Unmarked.
$40-50. *Right)* Unmarked. $45-65.

151

Fig. 574. *Left)* Unmarked. $45-60. *Right)* Unmarked. $45-60.

Fig. 575. *Left)* Marked – Fedora. $45-60. *Right)* Unmarked. $45-55.

Fig. 576. Ironstone, probably English. *Left)* Unmarked. $45-55. *Right)* Unmarked. $35-45.

Fig. 577. Ironstone, probably English. *Left)* Unmarked. $35-45. *Center)* Unmarked. $20-30. *Right)* Unmarked. $25-35.

Fig. 578. Ironstone, probably English. *Left)* Unmarked. $25-35. *Right)* Hand painted. Unmarked. $30-45.

Fig. 580. *Left)* Two handles, King Tut feature. Unmarked. $25-40. *Right)* Applied flowers. Unmarked. $25-35.

Fig. 579. *Left)* Hand painted. Unmarked. $35-45. *Right)* Lefton China. Marked – crown, Lefton China, Hand painted. Importer's mark, George Lefton Company, manufactured in Japan, c. 1950. $20-30.

Fig. 581 *Left)* Boat scene. Unmarked. $35-45. *Center)* Blown-out flower in mold. Unmarked. $20-30. *Right)* Tapestry, made to copy Royal Bayreuth. Well done, but not as high of quality. Unmarked. $45-65.

153

Fig. 582. *Left)* Beautiful gold work. Unmarked. $35-40. *Center)* Two handles. Unmarked. $45-60. *Right)* Very thin porcelain. Unmarked. $30-45.

Fig. 583. *Left)* Pink floral. Unmarked. $35-45 *Right)* Beautiful hand painted. Possibly Limoges. Unmarked. $35-45

Fig. 584. *Left)* Very thin, hand painted porcelain. Unmarked. $30-40. *Center)* Egg shaped, applied flowers. Unmarked. $25-35. *Right)* Hand painted floral. Unmarked. $35-45.

Fig. 585. *Left)* Hand painted floral. Unmarked. $45-55. *Right)* Raised gold rim. Unmarked. $30-45.

Fig. 586. *Left)* Hand painted square. Unmarked. $35-45. *Center)* Unusual finish, black is satin, scene is gloss. Unmarked. $30-40. *Right)* Raised flower design. Unmarked. $35-50.

Fig. 587. High quality porcelain. Unmarked. $35-45.

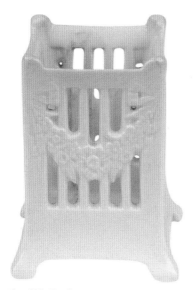

Fig. 588. Parian ware. Unmarked. $30-40.

Fig. 589. *Left)* Bisque. Unmarked. $25-35. *Right)* Bisque. Unmarked. $20-30.

Fig. 590. *Left)* Phoenix Bird. Unmarked. $45-55. *Right)* Floral. Unmarked. $45-55.

Fig. 591. *Left)* Hand painted. Unmarked. $25-35. *Right)* Good mold detail. Unmarked. $25-35.

Contemporary Toothpick Holders

The contemporary toothpicks shown in this chapter are the type sold to china decorators. We urge you to become familiar with these shapes so you will be able to distinguish a new toothpick from an old one. Many of the newer ones are beautifully decorated and would be an asset to any collection. However, you should know what you are buying and the items should be priced accordingly.

We have made no attempt to include the many, inexpensive ceramic and pottery toothpicks that are readily available in grocery stores and gift shops.

Fig. 592. Similar, but different molds. *Left)* Square base, four small feet, hand painted, artist signed "Vera (Haverfield) 1993." $25-35. *Right)* Slightly wider, round base, four small feet, hand painted, artist signed "Irving, Tex 1980 NTHCS by Omans." $25-35.

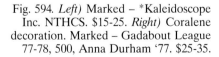

Fig. 593. Contemporary mold, hand painted. Unmarked. $15-25.

Fig. 594. *Left)* Marked – *Kaleidoscope Inc. NTHCS. $15-25. *Right)* Coralene decoration. Marked – Gadabout League 77-78, 500, Anna Durham '77. $25-35.

Fig. 595. *Left)* Hand painted, sanitary.
$15-25. *Right)* Hand painted. $15-25.

Fig. 596. *Left)* Contemporary toothpick with fake Nippon mark.
See Fig. 294. $25-30. *Right)* Hand painted, Unmarked. $15-25.

Match Holders

There were many match holders produced using a toothpick mold and vise versa. To identify a match holder, there is an area either on the bottom or some portion of the mold that has ridges or a rough texture. This is referred to as a "striker" and was used for lighting matches. We show a representative sample of shapes that were also made as toothpick holders.

Fig. 597. Examples of strikers – concentric circles, wavy ridges, and straight ridges.

Fig. 598. *Left)* Unusual Jester in flower transfer, trumpet on reverse side, striker on bottom. Unmarked. $25-35. *Right)* Striker on bottom. Unmarked. $20-30.

Fig. 599. *Left)* Marked – Lichtenberg Germany. $20-30. *Center)* Striker on bottom. Unmarked. $20-30. *Right)* Same mold as left, shows striker on side. Marked – Lichtenberg Germany. $20-30.

Fig. 600. *Left)* Unmarked. $25-35. *Center)* Unmarked. $25-35. *Right)* Unmarked. $20-30.

Fig. 601. *Left)* Unmarked. $25-35. *Right)* Unmarked. $30-40.

160

Fig. 602. *Left)* Striker on bottom. Unmarked $25-45. *Right)* Striker on bottom. Marked – JPL France. $30-40.

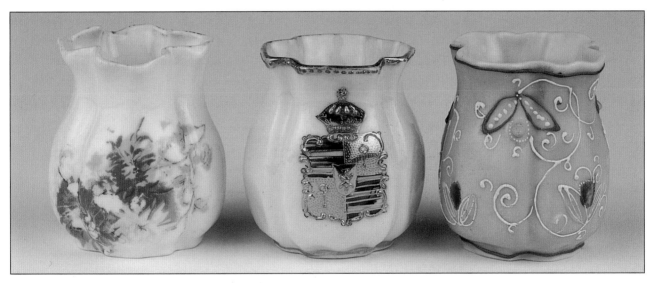

Fig. 603. *Left)* Marked – see Fig. 604. $20-30. *Center)* Unmarked. $20-30. *Right)* Unmarked. $30-40.

Fig. 604. Victoria Porcelain Factory, c. 1904-1918.

Appendix
Prussia Drawings

The line drawings in this appendix show the variety of molds produced by the various Schegelmilch-related factories. Since the decorations sometimes conceal mold details, these drawings may be useful in identifying unmarked Prussia molds. The older molds are shown first. The drawings are labeled with the figure number that corresponds to a photograph of the toothpick in this reference.

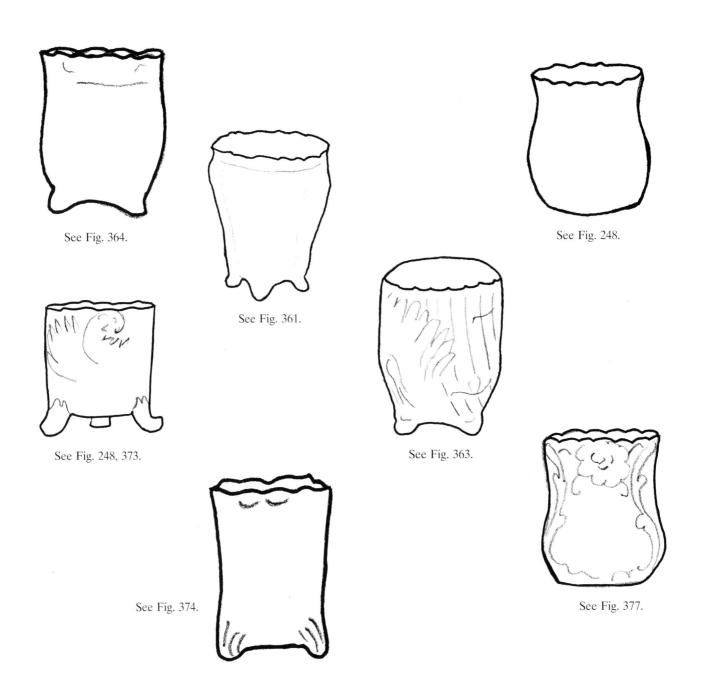

See Fig. 364.

See Fig. 361.

See Fig. 248.

See Fig. 248, 373.

See Fig. 363.

See Fig. 374.

See Fig. 377.

No example.

See Fig. 403.

See Fig. 371.

See Fig. 369.

See Fig. 388.

See Fig. 373.

See Fig. 373.

See Fig. 370.

See Fig. 390.

See Fig. 375.

See Fig. 360.

See Fig. 374.

See Fig. 360.

No example.

See Fig. 366.

See Fig. 363.

See Fig. 365.

No example.

See Fig. 383, 390.

See Fig. 283.

See Fig. 367.

See Fig. 391.

See Fig. 383.

No example.

See Fig. 367.

See Fig. 382.

See Fig. 380.

See Fig. 366.

See Fig. 369.

See Fig. 368.

See Fig. 378.

See Fig. 268.

See Fig. 372.

See Fig. 423.

See Fig. 368.

See Fig. 379.

See Fig. 374.

See Fig. 224.

See Fig. 381.

See Fig. 391.

See Fig. 382.

See Fig. 390.

See Fig. 410.

See Fig. 411.

See Fig. 428.

See Fig. 426.

See Fig. 411.

See Fig. 407.

See Fig. 393, 394.

See Fig. 402.

See Fig. 410.

See Fig. 389.

See Fig. 376, 377.

See Fig. 396.

See Fig. 377.

See Fig. 418.

See Fig. 404, 405.

See Fig. 4, 388.

See Fig. 423, 424.

See Fig. 398.

See Fig. 401.

See Fig. 424, 425.

See Fig. 425.

See Fig. 397, 398.

See Fig. 400.

See Fig. 396, 397.

See Fig. 401.

See Fig. 394, 395.

See Fig. 387.

See Fig. 399, 435.

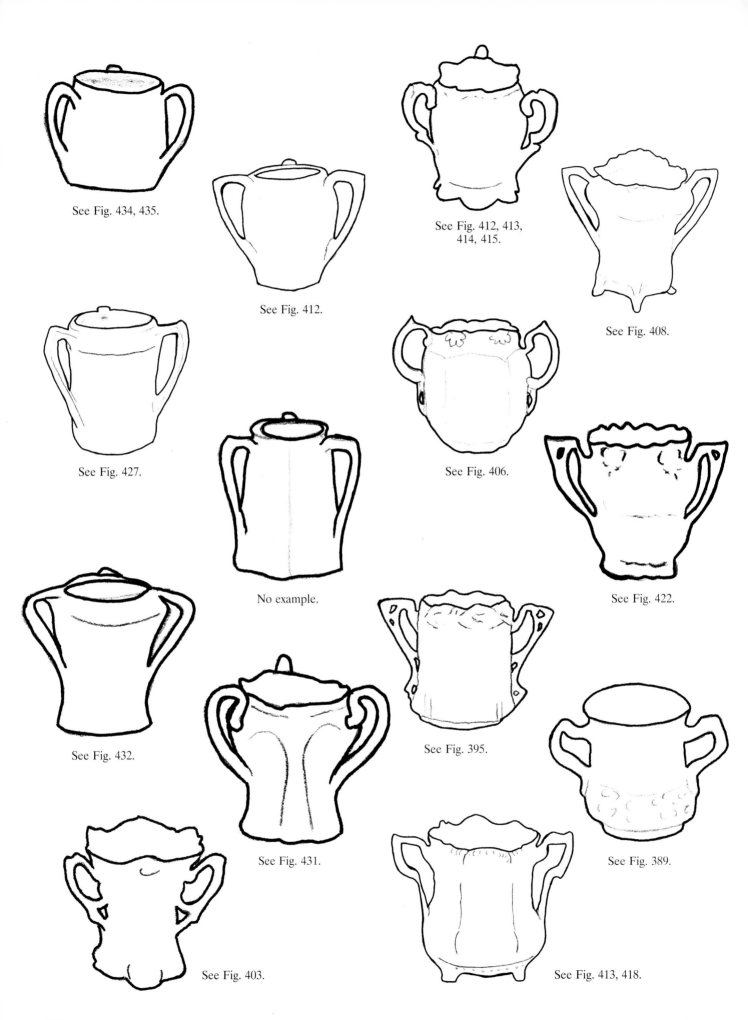

See Fig. 434, 435.

See Fig. 412.

See Fig. 412, 413,
414, 415.

See Fig. 408.

See Fig. 427.

See Fig. 406.

See Fig. 422.

No example.

See Fig. 432.

See Fig. 395.

See Fig. 389.

See Fig. 431.

See Fig. 403.

See Fig. 413, 418.

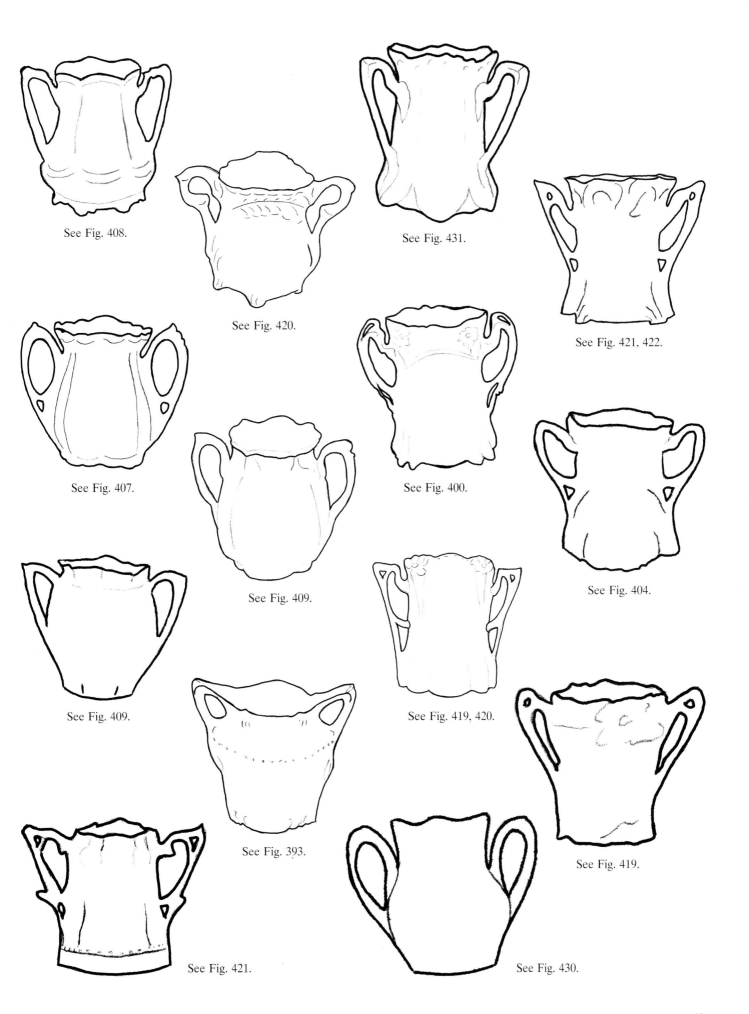

See Fig. 408.

See Fig. 420.

See Fig. 431.

See Fig. 421, 422.

See Fig. 407.

See Fig. 409.

See Fig. 400.

See Fig. 404.

See Fig. 409.

See Fig. 393.

See Fig. 419, 420.

See Fig. 419.

See Fig. 421.

See Fig. 430.

See Fig. 437.

See Fig. 429.

See Fig. 433.

See Fig. 426.

See Fig. 433.

See Fig. 406.

See Fig. 436.

See Fig. 430.

See Fig. 429.

See Fig. 392.

See Fig. 392.

See Fig. 432.

See Fig. 436.

See Fig. 428.

Glossary

Backstamp. A manufacturer's or importer's name or mark, or the name of a country, stamped on the bottom of a porcelain item.

Bavaria. A state in Germany known for its production of fine china.

Bisque. Unglazed porcelain. Also called biscuit.

Blanks. Undecorated pieces of china. Sometimes called "white china."

Bone China. A variety of fine, naturally white porcelain developed by English potters in the last half of the 18th and early 19th century. The clay is tempered with phosphate of lime or bone ash, increasing the strength of the porcelain during and after firing. Also called bone porcelain.

Carnival Lustre. Author's name for a unique type of German porcelain that is decorated by adding porcelain molded in the shape of ruffles, braids, twists, etc. to the basic blank before decorating. The same blank can be found with different applied decorations. Often decorated with gold and dark colors such as blue and purple, then given a lustre finish.

Ceramic. A general term for products made from clay and fired at a high temperature. Today, commonly used to refer to inexpensive, highly porous pieces of china.

China. A translucent ceramic material, biscuit-fired at a high temperature, its glaze fired at a low temperature. General term applied to any porcelain ware.

Clay. Common name for a number of fine-grained, earthy materials that become plastic when wet. Comes from the ground, usually in areas where streams or rivers once flowed. How far silt travels from its source and how pure the silt is determines the type of clay it becomes.

Decal. A picture or design created on special paper so it can be removed and applied (transferred) to another article. Also see Transfer.

Delft. An earthenware having an opaque white glaze with an overglaze decoration, usually in blue. The name delft is also often applied to wares of a similar nature.

Earthenware. A type of common clay that may contain some sand or small bits of rock. Earthenware is a secondary clay. Because of its many impurities, earthenware melts at a cooler temperature than other clays. After firing, it is still porous and—unless glazed—is often white or gray.

Elfinware. Porcelain decorated with applied raised porcelain flowers and green fillagree. Made primarily in Germany. Pieces marked "Elfinware Made in Germany" were generally imported after 1945.

Embossed. Raised in relief from the surface. Beading, scrollwork, and other designs were incorporated into the mold.

Fairyland Lustre. Commonly refers to a type of ware produced by Wedgwood with a unique lustre and a mottled appearance. Decorations such as dragons, butterflies, and birds were added to both the exterior and the interior. The inside of the items is also decorated. (Originally referred to items decorated in vivid colors depicting fairy-like characters and given a lustre finish.)

Fake. A contemporary item that looks like a desirable collectible or antique and can easily be mistaken for the genuine article. A contemporary item bearing a mark known to have been used to identify an authentic collectible or antique.

Figural. A decorative item in the shape of a person, animal, or thing.

Glaze. A translucent layer that coats pottery to give the surface a finish or provide a ground for decorative painting. Glazes—transparent, white, or colored—are fired on the clay. The coloring agents are oxides of different metals. Salt Glaze is a ceramic glaze on stoneware produced by the chemical reaction that occurs when salt is thrown into a kiln during firing.

Hard paste. Porcelain made with a larger portion of kaolin and fired to a temperature where it becomes completely nonporous. When tapped, the sound is a resounding ring. Most porcelain from Germany, Bohemia, and Austria is hard paste.

Iridescent. A surface finish that reflects a play of colors creating a rainbow-like effect.

Ironstone. A heavy, durable white china developed in England early in the 19th century. Often used for restaurant ware.

Kaolin. The purest clay, it is also called "china clay." It is a primary clay, found very near its source and has few impurities. It is the main ingredient used in making porcelain. Because its particle size is larger than other clays, it is not very plastic. This means that in a moist unfired state, kaolin tears when it is bent. Porcelain made from Kaolin is fired at such high temperatures that it can become very hard and translucent, its melted surface becoming so smooth and shiny that a glaze is not needed.

Limoges. An area in France known for the production of fine china dinnerware. Home to many porcelain factories.

Lithopane. Also spelled lithophane. A transparency made of varying thicknesses of porcelain or bone china, having an intaglio design. The designs are made more distinct by transmitted light.

Lustre. An iridescent metallic film produced on the surface of a ceramic glaze. Pottery with an overglaze finish containing copper and silver or other materials that give the effect of iridescence. It was sometimes used to enhance majolica. In England the technique came into vogue in the 19th century and was utilized by Josiah Wedgwood and Josiah Spode.

Majolica. A tin-glazed earthenware usually associated with wares produced in Spain, Italy, and Mexico, although some was made in the US. The process of making majolica consists of first firing a piece of earthenware, then applying a tin enamel that upon drying forms a white opaque porous surface. A design is then painted on and a transparent glaze applied. Finally the piece is fired again.

Matte. A smooth, but lusterless finish.

Mold. A form used to create or shape an item. Also used to refer to the shape of the item that is molded.

Moriage. A raised decoration formed of slip clay applied to porcelain, giving it a very textured feel. A Japanese technique.

Nippon. A name designating Japanese import ware produced between the years of 1891 and 1921. Wares produced prior to 1891 were either not marked or marked with Japanese characters. The official country of origin was changed from Nippon, the Japanese name for Japan, to Japan in 1921.

Occupied Japan. Items exported from Japan during the occupation that followed World War II were marked "Made in Japan" or "Occupied Japan" (1945-1952).

Old Ivory. A type of decoration applied to china made by Hermann Ohme, Silesia. Exterior is a matte cream color decorated with subdued colors, mostly floral designs. Trim is done in brown and gold. Many companies copied this style and some labeled their wares "Old Ivory."

Overglaze. A color or glaze applied to an existing glaze, or a decoration or mark applied to a ceramic object over an existing glaze.

Pearlized. A surface finish with a soft pearl-like lustre that reflects a rainbow of pastel colors.

Porcelain. A white, hard, permanent, nonporous pottery having translucence, and which is resonant when struck. Porcelain is a strong, vitreous, translucent ceramic material, produced by firing biscuit at a low temperature and then firing the glaze at a very high temperature. Made from kaolin clay.

Pottery. The baked-clay wares of the entire ceramics field. It usually falls into three main classes—porous-bodied pottery, stoneware, and porcelain. Fired pottery, unlike sun-dried clay, retains a permanent shape and does not disintegrate in water. Stoneware is produced by raising the temperature, and porcelain is baked at still greater heat.

Reissue. An item put back into production after not being offered for many years. This is often done by the same company that originally produced the item.

Reproduction. An item made recently that is similar to an older or antique item.

Sanded. A textured finish that resembles sand.

Satsuma. A Japanese pottery from Kyushu, first produced in the early 17th century and after 1800 having a crackle glaze and overglaze enameling and gilding.

Silesia. At one time, a region in Germany.

Slip. A mixture of clay and water that can be colored and applied to the surface of pottery. Slipware refers to pottery that is decorated with slip, such as Moriage.

Soft paste. Porcelain made with a smaller portion of kaolin and not fired to the point where it becomes completely nonporous. When tapped, the sound is short and dull. Most porcelain from China and Japan is soft paste.

Striker. Ridges or a rough area on the side or bottom of a holder that could be used for striking a match. Strikers distinguish an item as a match holder rather than a toothpick holder, even though the same mold was often used.

Tapestry. A linen-like finish achieved by dipping coarse fabric in slip and then wrapping it around an item before firing. The fabric is burned away in the firing. The item is then re-fired and decorated.

Toothpicks. An abbreviated name for "toothpick holders" commonly used among collectors and dealers.

Transfer. A decal applied to china as a means of decorating the item.

Transfer ware. China decorated by the application of a transfer or a decal, as opposed to being painted or decorated in some other way.

Translucent. Permits the passage of light. You can determine how translucent an item is by holding it to the light and moving your hand behind it.

Underglaze. Refers to a color, decoration, or mark that is applied to a piece before the piece is glazed.

Bibliography

Alden, Aimee Neff. *Collector's Encyclopedia of Early Noritake*. Paducah, Kentucky: Collector Books, 1995.

Capers, R.H. *Capers' Notes on the Marks of Prussia*. El Paso, Illinois: Alphabet Printing, Inc., 1996.

Dale, Jean. *The Charlton Standard Catalogue of Royal Doulton Beswick Jugs, 3rd Edition*. Birmingham, Michigan: The Charlton Press, 1995.

Gaston, Mary Frank. *Collector's Encyclopedia of Limoges*. Paducah, Kentucky: Collector Books, 1994.

Gaston, Mary Frank. *Collector's Encyclopedia of R .S. Prussia - 1st Series*. Paducah, Kentucky: Collector Books, 1982.

Gaston, Mary Frank. *Collector's Encyclopedia of R. S. Prussia – 2nd Series*. Paducah, Kentucky: Collector Books, 1986.

Gaston, Mary Frank. *Collector's Encyclopedia of R. S. Prussia – 3rd Series*. Paducah, Kentucky: Collector Books, 1994.

Gaston, Mary Frank. *Collector's Encyclopedia of R. S. Prussia – 4th Series*. Paducah, Kentucky: Collector Books, 1995.

Gaston, Mary Frank. *R.S. Prussia Popular Lines*. Paducah, Kentucky: Collector Books, 1999.

Heacock, William. *1000 Toothpick Holders, A collector's Guide*. Marietta, Ohio: Antique Publications, 1977.

Henderson, James D. Dr. *Bohemian Decorated Porcelain*. Atglen, Pennsylvania: Schiffer Publishing Ltd., 1999.

Hillman, Alma, David Goldschmitt, and Adam Szynkiewicz. *Old Ivory China*. Paducah, Kentucky: Collector Books, 1998.

Husfloen, Kyle, Ed., *Antique Trader Antiques & Collectibles 2002 Price Guide*. Iola, Wisconsin: Krause Publications, 2001.

Kamm, Dorothy. *American Painted Porcelain*. Paducah, Kentucky: Collector Books, 1999.

Kovel, Ralph and Terry. *Kovels' Illustrated Price Guide to Royal Doulton*. New York, New York: Crown Publishers, 1980.

Kovel, Ralph and Terry. *Kovels' New Dictionary of Marks*. New York, New York: Crown Publishers, 1986.

Marple, Leland and Carol. *R. S. Prussia; The Art Nouveau Years*. Atglen, Pennsylvania: Schiffer Publishing Ltd., 1998.

Marple, Leland and Carol. *R. S. Prussia; The Early Years*. Atglen, Pennsylvania: Schiffer Publishing Ltd., 1997.

Marple, Leland and Carol. *R. S. Prussia; The Formative Years*. Atglen, Pennsylvania: Schiffer Publishing Ltd., 2002.

Marple, Leland and Carol. *R. S. Prussia; The Wreath and the Star*. Atglen, Pennsylvania: Schiffer Publishing Ltd., 2000.

McCaslin, Mary J. *Royal Bayreuth; A Collector's Guide*. Marietta, Ohio: Antique Publications, 1994.

McCaslin, Mary J. *Royal Bayreuth; A Collector's Guide - Book II*. Marietta, Ohio: Antique Publications, 2000.

National Toothpick Holder Collector's Society. *Toothpick Holders: China, Glass and Metal*. Marietta, Ohio: Antique Publications, 1992.

Ormsbee, Thomas H. *English China and its Marks*. New York, New York: Hearthside Press, Inc., 1959.

Petersen, A. and E. Paul. *Collector's Handbook to Marks on Porcelain and Pottery*. Greens Farms, Connecticut: Modern Books and Crafts, Inc., 1974.

Reed, Alan B. *Collector's Encyclopedia of Pickard China*. Paducah, Kentucky: Collector Books, 2000.

Rontgen, Robert E. *Marks on German, Bohemian and Austrian Porcelain: 1710 to Present. Updated and Revised Edition*. Atglen, Pennsylvania: Schiffer Publishing Ltd., 1997.

Spain, David. *Noritake Collectibles A to Z*. Atglen, Pennsylvania: Schiffer Publishing Ltd., 2000.

Schroeder's Antiques Price Guide. Paducah, Kentucky: Collector Books, 1993.

Van Patten, Joan F. *Collectors Encyclopedia of Nippon Porcelain: Series 6 Identification & Values*. Paducah, Kentucky: Collector Books, 2000.

Williams, Laurence. W. *Collector's Guide to Souvenir China*. Paducah, Kentucky: Collector Books, 1998.

Williams, Peter. *Wedgwood: A Collector's Guide*. Radnor, Pennsylvania: Wallace-Homestead Book Company, 1992.

Index

Figure numbers shown in *italics*.

A

Alice, *Fig. 14, 27*
Arabs (RB), *Fig. 93-95*
Arcadia China, *Fig. 169, 170*
Austria, 18, 49, 66; *Fig. 4, 5-12*
Aynsley, *Fig. 150, 152, 174*

B

Babes in the Woods, 23
Banks & Biddles, *Fig. 208*
Bauscher Porcelain, *Fig. 497*
Bauser & Weiden, *Fig. 498*
Bavaria, 14, 19; *Fig. 3, 13-30, 487-491*
Bawo & Dotter, 49; *Fig. 9, 10*
Bell Ringer (RB), *Fig. 70*
Belleek, Irish, *Fig. 456, 553-554*
Beyer & Bock, *Fig. 438, 455*
Bing & Grondahl, *Fig. 546-548*
Bisque. *Fig. 281, 512, 515, 519, 525, 529, 535, 539, 588-589*
Blue Onion, 23; *Fig. 123, 492, 572-573*
Bohemia, 49; *Fig. 140*
Bohne, Ernest, *Fig. 525-527*
Brittany Women (RB), *Fig. 110, 111*
Burley & Tyrrell Co., *Fig. 133*

C

Cacilie, *Fig. 14, 15, 27*
Capo-di-monte, *Fig. 556-557*
Carlsbad, *Fig. 5*
Carmen, 72; *Fig. 21, 28, 234*
Carnival Lustre, 11, 75, 86; *Fig. 286-291*
Carsten, C&E, *Fig. 215, 217-219,, 235*
Ceramic Art Co., *Fig. 456-457*
Charlotte, *Fig. 15, 27*
CHIC USA, *Fig. 347*
China, *Fig. 545*
Clarion, 72; *Fig. 234*
Classic (see Corinthian Ware),
Clown (RB), *Fig. 71*
Coachman (RB), *Fig. 72*
Coalport, *Fig. 157*
Condiment set, 8; *Fig. 229, 309, 322*
Contemporary, 5, 14, 87, 157; *Fig. 3, 358, 592-596*
Copeland, *Fig. 145, 172*

Copper, Lustre *Fig. 563, 565*
Corinthian Ware, 23; *Fig. 126, 127*
Count Thun, 49
Crown Staffordshire, *Fig. 159, 177*
Czechoslovakia, 49, 66; *Fig. 137-143, 492*

D

Decorating, 10-11
Delft, German, *Fig. 230, 241*
Delphine China, *Fig. 157*
Denmark, *Fig. 485, 546-548*
Derby Porcelain Works, *Fig. 153-155, 175*
Derwent China, *Fig. 169*
Devil, *Fig. 73, 82, 535*
Dickens Ware, 59; *Fig. 179-181, 183*
Dresden, *Fig. 156, 176, 213-215, 236, 472*
Dudson, *Fig. 166, 167*
Duppel-Mohle, *Fig. 518*
Dutch Children (RB), 23; *Fig. 48-55*

E

EAM Co., *Fig. 458-459*
Eglantine, 72; *Fig. 231, 234*
Elfinware, 11, 75, 87; *Fig. 292-293*
Elite, *Fig. 206, 212*
Elk (RB), *Fig. 74*
Elysee, 72
England, 51; *Fig. 144-199, 493-495, 505, 566, 576-578*
Etiquette, 8

F

Fairyland Lustre, *Fig. 146-149, 173*
Fakes, 14, 87, 102; *Fig. 294, 358-359, 596*
Figurals, 5, 23, 33, 137; *Fig. 70-85 (RB), 372, 511-544*
Florette, 72
Flow Blue, *Fig. 263*
France, 63; *Fig. 200-212, 496, 566, 602*

G

Geisha Girl, 87; *Fig. 295-297*
Germany, 7, 66; *Fig. 213-293, 497-499, 524-527, 540-544, 599*
Germany, R. S. (also see Prussia), 60, 102; *Fig. 412, 434-437, 446, 569*
Guerin, *Fig. 211-212*

Giraud, *Fig. 205*
Glaze, 10-11
Glossary, 171
Gobelin, *Fig. 136*
Goss, *Fig. 168-170*
Greece, *Fig. 500*

H

Hammersley, *Fig. 156, 171*
Haviland, 63; *Fig. 208*
HC Royal, *Fig. 223*
Heinrich & Co., *Fig. 487-488*
Holland, *Fig. 549-551*
Horizontal, (see Sanitary)
Horn, H. Wehinger, *Fig. 9, 11*
Horse Head (RB), *Fig. 75*
Hungary, *Fig. 552*
Hunt, B. F. & Sons, 127
Hutschenreuther, 19; *Fig. 20, 27*

I

Imperial Nippon, 87; *Fig. 329, 337*
Insurance, 15
Inventory, 13
Ireland, *Fig. 553-555*
Ironstone, 51; *Fig. 576-578*
Italy, *Fig. 556-557*

J

Jaeger & Company, *Fig. 15, 490-491*
Japan, 87; *Fig. 4, 294-357, 519, 531, 537, 596*
Jasperware, *Fig. 165, 167, 280*
Jester, *Fig. 128 (RB), 598*
JHR & Co., *Fig. 482-483*

K

Kampfe & List Porcelain, *Fig. 218, 222, 237*
Krister Porcelain (KPM), *Fig. 228-229, 240, 462*
Klemm, Richard, *Fig. 214*

L

Lamp Lighter (RB), *Fig. 76*
Lefton China, *Fig. 579*
Lenox, *Fig. 456*
Leonard, P. H., 49; *Fig. 8*
Limoges, 63; *Fig. 200-206, 211-212, 496, 583*
Lithopane (also spelled lithophane), *Fig. 558-559*
Lobster and Lettuce (RB), *Fig. 77*
Longwy Pottery, *Fig. 566*
Lustre, 11; *Fig. 146-149, 173, 204, 221-222, 255, 275, 278-291, 305, 321-322, 503, 533, 563, 565*

M

Madeleine, *Fig. 20, 28*
Majolica, *Fig. 509-510, 560-562*
Malmaison, *Fig. 23, 28*
Maple Leaf mark, 87; *Fig. 294, 342*
Marktredwitz, *Fig. 15, 490-491*
Match holders, 159; *Fig. 597-604*
Meakin, Alfred, *Fig. 505*
Meito China, *Fig. 315, 357*
Mitterteich Porcelain, *Fig. 478-479*
Monbijou, *Fig. 20, 28*
Moriage, *Fig. 323-324*
Moritz Zdekauer, *Fig. 5-6*
Moriumra Bros., 87; *Fig. 304-306, 313-314, 342, 349-351*
Muff Children (RB), *Fig. 56*
Mustershutz, *Fig. 143*

N

NationalToothpickHolderCollectors Society (NTHCS), 12, 14, 15
Nelsonware, *Fig. 164*
Nippon. (see Japan)
Nodder. *Fig. 513*
Noritake. *Fig. 315, 317, 350*
Noke, Charles. 59; *Fig. 128, 187*
Nursery Rhymes (RB), 23; *Fig. 57-62*

O

Ohme, Hermann, 72; *Fig. 231, 233-234, 242, 244, 516*
Old Ivory, 10, 72; *Fig. 90 (RB), 231, 233-234, 244*
Olimpic, *Fig. 216*
Overglaze, 11
Oyster Pearl (RB), *Fig. 78*

P

Pansy (RB), *Fig. 79*
Parian ware, *Fig. 588*
Pickard,124; *Fig. 460-465, 569*
Pink Pigs, 144 *Fig. 540-544*
Portraits, *Fig. 23, 107-109, 116-117, 278-279, 385-386*
Pouyat, Jean, *Fig. 201-202, 206-207, 211-212*
Pricing, 16
Prov Saxe, *Fig. 372, 389, 392, 452*
Prussia, 5, 102; *Fig. 4, 137, 222, 224, 227, 238, 248, 262, 268-269, 278-279, 283, 285, 289, 358-455, 476, Appendix A*

Q

Quadrille, 72

R

Red Pepper (RB), *Fig. 83*
Reproductions, 14, 102; *Fig. 3*
Richter, *Fig. 3, 11, 17*
Ridgeway, *Fig. 494*
Rogers-Martini Co., *Fig. 437*
Rose (RB), *Fig. 83*
Rose Tapestry, 23; *Fig. 86-87*
Rosenthal, 19; *Fig. 21-23, 28*
Royal Bayreuth, 5, 10, 23; *Fig. 31, 32-136, 571-572, 581*
Royal Blue Medallion, *Fig. 524*
Royal Ceramic (RC), *Fig. 345*
Royal Copenhagen, *Fig. 123, 572*
Royal Crest Porcelain, *Fig. 466-467*
Royal Crown Derby, *Fig. 153-155, 175*
Royal Doulton, 59; *Fig. 179-199*
Royal Rothenburg, *Fig. 482-483*
Royal Rudolstadt, *Fig. 438, 455*
Royal Satsuma, 87; *Fig. 330, 338*
Royal Silesia, 102; *Fig. 448*
Royal Tillowitz, 102; *Fig. 433*
Royal Vienna, 102
Royal Winton, *Fig. 151*
Royal Worcester, *Fig. 160-163, 178*

S

Sand Babies (RB), 23; *Fig. 66*
Sanitary, 131; *Fig. 486-510*
SAXE ALTENBURG, Fig. *443*
Schafer & Vater, *Fig. 517*
Schlegelmilch, 102; Also see Prussia
Schlegelmilch, Carl, 102; *Fig. 453*
Schlegelmilch, Erdmann, 102; *Fig. 362, 379, 385-386, 389, 449-452*
Schlegelmilch, Oscar, 102; *Fig. 368, 377, 454*
Schlegelmilch, Reinhold, 102; *Fig. 4, 285, 358-359, 439-448*
Schmidt & Co., *Fig. 140, 492*
Schonwald, *Fig. 23, 29*
Seltmann, *Fig. 24, 30*
Shelley China, *Fig. 158*
Shofu, *Fig. 308, 355*
Silesia, 72; *Fig. 231-234, 240, 499, 516*
Slip, 10
Snow Babies (RB), 22; *Fig. 67*
Souvenir, 127; *Fig. 311, 387, 469-485*

Spiny Shell (RB), *Fig. 85*
Spode, *Fig. 145, 172*
Stouffer, J. H., *Fig. 460-461*
Suhl, *Fig. 450, 452*
Sunbonnet Babies (RB), 22; *Fig. 63-65*
Swaine & Co., *Fig. 230, 241*
Sydney British Anchor, *Fig. 495*
Syracuse China, *Fig. 468, 484*

T

Tapestry, 23; *Fig. 31, 40, 86, 87, 107, 109, 117, 121, 122, 581*
Tettau, 23; *Fig. 123*
Three Crown China, 72; *Fig. 226-228, 232-233, 243*
Tielsch, C & Co., *Fig. 499*
Tillowitz, R. S., *Fig. 433, 445*
Tilly, *Fig. 21, 28*
Tirschenreuth, *Fig. 26*
Top Hat, *Fig. 386, 522-523, 543*
Torquay Pottery, *Fig. 566*
Transfer, 10
Turnivals, *Fig. 157*

U

Underglaze, 11
United Porcelain Factory, *Fig. 142*
United States, 124; *Fig. 456-467*

V

Victoria Porcelain Factory, *Fig. 604*
Vienna, 49
Vohenstrauss, *Fig. 30*

W

Wade, *Fig. 536, 555*
Wegdwood, *Fig. 144, 146-149, 173, 280*
Weiden, *Fig. 497, 498*
Weimar, (see Carsten, C&E)
Wheelock, 127; *Fig. 469, 472, 480*
World's Fair, *Fig. 311*

Z

Zdekauer, *Fig. 6*